IESTYN HARRIS:
THERE AND BACK

I'd like to dedicate this book to the two most important people in my life, my beautiful daughter, Catrin Elizabeth, and my unborn son, Cameron Rhys. Daddy loves you!

IESTYN HARRIS

Iestyn Harris

My Journey from League to Union and Back Again

MAINSTREAM
PUBLISHING
EDINBURGH AND LONDON

First published in Great Britain in 2005 by
MAINSTREAM PUBLISHING COMPANY
(EDINBURGH) LTD
7 Albany Street
Edinburgh EH1 3UG

ISBN 1 84596 001 7

A catalogue record for this book is available from the
British Library

Typeset in Giovanni and TradeGothic

Printed and bound in Great Britain by
William Clowes Ltd, Beccles, Suffolk

CONTENTS

ONE

GOING BACK

In the summer of 2004, I should have been on my first overseas tour with Wales to Argentina and South Africa under new coach Mike Ruddock. Instead, I decided on another monumental upheaval – to go back to rugby league.

I had an injury which prevented me from going on that tour, so I ended up going on holiday with my wife Becky and spending most of the time talking over my future. When we returned, we'd made the decision to move back up north.

I had no idea, however, that my signing for the Bradford Bulls would lead to legal action being taken against me and the Bulls by the Leeds Rhinos, my former club. This hung over me for the next 12 months, the case eventually ending up at the High Court in London.

In addition to this controversy, my move back to league led to quite a bit of debate and even provoked criticism from one of my idols, Jonathan Davies. Jonathan had achieved legendary status both in rugby union and rugby league; in fact, I took his place when I made my debut for Warrington at the age of 17.

I was coming up to 28 and my career was at a crossroads. I'd achieved so much already. As a youngster born and brought up in

Oldham, I had always wanted to be a professional rugby player and, where I grew up, that meant rugby league.

On the other hand, I had a Welsh father and a grandfather who had been a rugby union international for Wales. I had always felt Welsh and dreamed of emulating the likes of Barry John and Phil Bennett by pulling on that famous number 10 jersey.

To achieve that, I'd turned my back on rugby league in 2001, leaving the Leeds Rhinos for Cardiff and Wales. Now, three years later, having played in the Six Nations and a World Cup, I felt I had to head back.

After that World Cup in 2003, I had every intention of staying in Wales for another 18 months. The contract I originally signed was for three years, with an option of another year, but by the start of 2004 I was thinking more and more about the future and what would be best for my family.

I know some people have said my mind was made up at the World Cup but that isn't true. I had always intended to sit down after the tour to Argentina and South Africa in the summer of 2004 and resolve my future. If I had been fit, I would have gone, no question. I had missed two Wales summer tours – to South Africa and to New Zealand and Australia – and was very disappointed to miss out for a third year in a row.

Going might have made a difference, as it would have given me the chance to work with Mike and who knows what might have happened if I had done that?

I had spoken to Mike at length and he was keen for me to tour. He pulled me in to see if there was any chance I could make it, even offering to play me in just one game! Mike was great and couldn't have done any more for me but in the end Mark Davies, the Wales physio, made the decision for me. I had damaged my knee ligaments against France in the Six Nations and they had troubled me for the rest of that season. I needed six weeks' rest to heal properly, so he decided I simply wasn't fit enough to go.

Becky and I went on holiday to the Turks and Caicos Islands in the Caribbean where we discussed the future for many hours. Eventually, we decided moving back was the right thing to do.

We had been talking about it for six months, going through all the pros and cons. We loved Cardiff, we loved the city and had made some really good friends there, so we knew the move would have its downside. However, we missed our family, and Catrin, our daughter, was missing her grandparents. In the end, being close to our family was the most important factor.

Another prominent reason was the impingement on my family life in Wales. I love the passion of the Welsh rugby fans and during my time there they were so supportive of me. But their commitment to the game and the fact that rugby union is the national sport in Wales made it a bit like living in a goldfish bowl. Since moving back to a small village near Oldham, my life has become so much easier because no one recognises me. In Wales, that's not the case and you're either a hero or a zero.

In England, there will be days when some newspapers don't carry any rugby at all but in Wales, a newspaper like the *Western Mail* has rugby every day, sometimes as many as five pages. I found that sort of high profile very hard to handle and when things weren't going very well it felt like I was on public trial. Of course I get paid well and can handle the criticism but it is harder to take when every bone in your body wants to succeed.

I don't mind talking to the media and I hope the press who've dealt with me over the years feel I've been fair and truthful with them, but what I can't accept is the intrusion into my private life that occurred when I was in Wales. I can't accept stories appearing about my marriage, for instance. The pressure of being in that kind of spotlight was certainly part of my reason for leaving union and returning to league. The best way you can describe it is that rugby in Wales is like football in England. You don't get a lot of privacy, you can't just go and do your shopping down a local supermarket and not get bothered, it's constant.

If Wales had played well and you had a good win, it was fantastic, everyone was friendly, tapping you on the back and happy to see you. The flip side was that if you had lost or played poorly, people treated you differently – you were the devil. All the Welsh players feel the same, it's very, very difficult to play for Wales and live in Wales. Sometimes I'd be out with my daughter and people would jump in between us. My little girl would be looking up as if to say, 'What's going on here, Dad?' I would have liked to continue in union but in the end my family had to come first.

Playing for Wales was fantastic but that only happend ten or eleven times a year, the rest was inconsistent rugby. I was missing the week-in-week-out intensity of Super League and this feeling gradually built up until I couldn't ignore it any more.

I was good friends with David Young, the Cardiff coach, and in constant contact with him. He knew the way I felt, that I was considering going back to league, and I kept him in the picture right up until the end. When I told him that I wouldn't be going back to Cardiff, he wished me all the best and I wished him well for the new season. Dai said an offer would be made to try to persuade me to stay but by that stage my mind had been made up.

As I wouldn't be taking up the option to return to Cardiff in September, it didn't make sense me being at the club with them paying my wages during the summer when there were no games. It was decided that I would go early and let my new club pay my wages. This was being negotiated when Cardiff released the statement to the effect that my contract had been terminated. This was the correct legal terminology for the agreement we had reached but I was disappointed with the way it came out.

I did go back to the club during the off-season with Bradford. I went down to see some friends in Cardiff and I popped my head around the door, watched a training session and had some lunch with them. I chatted to Dai and all the players, and I am still friends with many of them.

Mike Ruddock said he was very disappointed to see me return to league, which I can obviously understand. He was, however, very dignified, wished me luck and said there would be no hard feelings: sentiments that I appreciated.

During the World Cup, I'd spoken to Scott Johnson, Wales assistant coach, who went on the Lions tour in an observational role, about the tour to New Zealand in 2005 and he'd told me that I had to be serious about my approach, as he felt I could make a big impact on that tour. A Lions tour is something special and I knew I'd have to give it my all if I wanted to make it.

When I moved to union, I had meetings with Graham Henry where he explained how integral I could be to his plans with Wales. I knew if I kept my form I would play for Wales; but there were, of course, no guarantees as far as the Lions were concerned, so while it was in my mind I couldn't really bring it into the decision-making process.

I did have the option of moving and still staying in union, and we did consider looking for a Premiership club in the north of England. I wouldn't have played for the Leeds Tykes but Sale was a possibility. My agent knew there would be interest from union clubs but the more we talked, the more we knew it had to be a league club. In the end, I didn't even speak to Sale.

I still enjoyed league, watched league and I knew that there would be clubs interested in signing me. That was an attraction in itself, knowing that I would still be wanted.

I know people will say the move was about the money but that just wasn't the case. I gather that some footballers move purely for financial gain but that has never been a motivating factor for me. I believe that if you make a decision to move in sport because of money it will invariably be a wrong decision. There are so many more important things in life. The truth is that I didn't make money by moving to union because I was offered a similar contract to the one I had in league. Again, when I returned to league, I wasn't on a higher salary.

If I had never made it as a professional rugby league player, I'm sure I would still be playing amateur rugby league. I'm not sure whether I could go back to the amateur game once my professional days are over but I would definitely be involved in the game if I hadn't made it as a professional. Even if I won the lottery, I would still carry on playing professional rugby league, although I know it might make my next contract negotiations a little harder!

When I decided to return, I was in a position to look around for a club. From the beginning, Bradford and Leeds were the main two contenders. Although I was the subject of an April Fool's joke when a news report linked me with a return to Warrington, I can categorically say there was no truth in that one. I don't know where it came from but I gather it was from a hoax fax.

I know the supporters and everyone at Leeds thought I would return there after my time in union but I never saw it that way. I know a lot was made of the contract I signed when I left the Rhinos but I never thought it would stand up in court. I was naive to sign something which said I'd have to come back to Leeds if I ever came back to rugby league. I accept that now. But I hope that even Leeds fans will understand that after deciding to return I needed the opportunity to talk to many different clubs and sign the deal that was right for me and my family.

As far as I was concerned, I was a free agent. When I moved to rugby union, Leeds terminated my contract and I wasn't tied to them. When you terminate a contract, you shouldn't be able to put clauses in. You can't sell a car and then, in three years' time, say you want it back, it doesn't work like that.

I did meet Gary Hetherington, the Leeds chief executive, on a number of occasions. The frustrating thing is that we negotiated over three or four meetings and never mentioned that clause in the contract. Sometimes it was just him and me but at other meetings Gareth Davies, my adviser, was present and nothing was mentioned about the clause or the contract. However, in the latter stages, when Gary realised I wasn't going to sign for Leeds, he said, 'We've got a contract with you.' I was 90 per cent down the line with Bradford and my view was that they couldn't make me do that.

During my time at Leeds, I'd had my run-ins with Gary. Back in 1998–99 we had a really physical, dominant side and I felt that if the right decisions had been made from the top, we could have gone on being successful for five to ten years, particularly with the youth set-up they had. But it all got messed around and people were cut from the team because they wanted an extra couple of thousand. I didn't want to trust my last four years of rugby to someone if I wasn't fully confident about what was going on.

My discussions with Gary more or less concentrated on finances, whereas in my dealings with Brian Noble, the coach of Bradford, we concentrated on the playing and coaching side and talked more about the game.

The Rhinos said that I'd been 'coerced' by Bradford into signing for them. But Bradford were excellent and stood by me all the way. Talking to them got me very excited about this new stage of my career. I owe a great debt to the Bradford chairman, Chris Caisley, who made sure nothing would come between me and the move to Odsal. And when I made my decision, there was no other offer on the table, so how could I have been coerced?

When I did sign for the Bulls, Chris said, 'We are grateful to the RFL [Rugby Football League] for its acceptance of Iestyn's registration. Whilst it was obvious that Iestyn is a contracted Bulls player, there was a lot of misinformation being disseminated which clouded one very simple question: which club had Iestyn signed a rugby league contract with?

'As far as we are concerned, that aspect of the matter is closed, although we are looking into the very serious associated matter of the defamatory comments made of our club yesterday by the chief executive of the Leeds Rhinos.'

To which Rhinos chief executive Gary Hetherington replied, 'We have learnt that a player contract has been lodged with the RFL to register Iestyn. He will not, therefore, become a Rhinos player despite his contractual obligations to do so. We will now be taking legal proceedings.' The matter dragged on and a couple of days before the play-off match against the Bulls at Headingley at the beginning of October, Leeds announced court proceedings against me and the Bulls.

At least Leeds accepted that there was no truth in the story that Bradford had coerced me into joining them from rugby union. They had to apologise to Bradford for that allegation but they were still claiming I was contractually bound to Leeds on my return to rugby league. A statement from Leeds summed things up at that time: 'Formal claims were made by Rhinos against Iestyn Harris for breach of contract and against Bulls for inducing breach of contract. Regrettably, both Iestyn and Bulls have rejected these claims and refused to negotiate with Rhinos. Rhinos are therefore issuing legal proceedings against Iestyn and Bulls. The public will draw their own conclusions on this matter and the court will decide the legal issues.'

I had a fantastic few years at Leeds and I have a lot of friends there, but I felt the right place for me was Bradford and the four-and-a-half-year contract I signed with them will take me up towards the end of my career.

I never intended to put anyone's back up, or anything like that. All I wanted to do was get on with my rugby league at a club of my choosing. I know that Gary Hetherington was very vocal in the press about me joining Bradford and I feel, as do my advisers, that a lot of of what he said was pretty uncalled for.

When the deal to take me to rugby union was done in 2001, Leeds got a really good deal, receiving £750,000 plus VAT. As negotiations hit a sticking point, things were added, one of which was a corporate box at the Millennium Stadium for three seasons, which was probably worth maybe £60,000 to £100,000, while the other was the clause that led to the court case. There was quite a lot of confusion at the time as it came in at the last minute. I was supposed to sign on 8 August but I only found out about it that day. The new clause caused a delay, pushing back the signing and the press conference by a day.

Basically, Leeds wanted a contract in place for the fourth year, so if I left Cardiff after the initial three years, I had to take this contract up and go back to them. It's something which I had not known before and it has led to a lot of confusion. There was still a lot of confusion on my side at half ten on the morning of the day I actually signed, with a press conference now scheduled for one o'clock.

There was a lot of frustration in the air and people were trying to push the deal through. The advice I got was just to sign and not worry about it, as it wouldn't be enforceable. I didn't think it was fair but the only option for me was to sign or else the deal wouldn't have gone through.

When the case eventually went to court in 2005, the judge didn't seem to know too much about sport or rugby league and he confused this fourth-year clause with a first refusal option, which it wasn't. Basically it was a post-dated contract, which meant that after the third year of my rugby union contract, I had a choice between staying in rugby union with Cardiff and Wales or going to Leeds. I couldn't do anything else or go anywhere else. My view was that this was unfair and I was being forced into something I might not have wanted to do. The court case could have gone either way, it depended on how the judge saw it.

We argued that it was a complete restriction of trade. He ruled it to be restriction of trade but a reasonable restriction. There were two separate cases, one against me and one against Bradford but the judge rolled it into one, which to me was a strange decision. I think having a QC helped their case.

We're not going to appeal because it could take a lot of time and a lot of money for something that could end with the same result, so I think it will go to a separate panel of judges to deem what's reasonable compensation. Leeds have to prove they suffered a loss in 2005, which is going to be tough for them seeing as they were at the top of Super League and Challenge Cup finalists. I think they will probably apply for their legal costs to be paid but it's up in the air at the moment.

From my point of view and those of Leeds and Bradford, it's something which is hanging in the air and needs to be sorted out so we can all get on with the rugby. To be honest, if I'd signed for Warrington or St Helens, I don't think it would have been a major issue but there's a lot of bad blood between Bradford and Leeds and I think that has been the main reason for the court case; I've just been caught in the middle.

Certainly, during May, June and July of 2005 it was really tough. Instead of playing and training then going home to relax and enjoy time with the family before going back to training fresh, it was training, playing, court case. Going to the solicitor's to deal with everything contractual and then going back to training was a real drag.

Gary Hetherington must have had to endure the same sort of things because he'd have had to put in as much work as I did and he must have been as fed up to the back teeth as I was. We all need to put it behind us.

Danny McGuire and Rob Burrow have come in at half-back for Leeds and been a revelation, so I can't really understand why Leeds were so keen to sign me again, anyway. It's a strange situation.

You see similar situations in many sports where a player doesn't want to play for a club. It's always better to let him go because who would want a player at their club who didn't want to be there? When I made my decision to go to Bradford, Leeds should have accepted that and moved on.

For me, the overriding reason for not going back to Leeds was that I didn't want to go back to the scene of those glory years. I also wasn't able to forget how disillusioned I had felt with Leeds in my final six months. I didn't feel they had kicked on or were going to at that time. I lost confidence in the way the club was run and with this being the last major move I would make, I had to ensure it would be exactly right for my playing future. I talked to Brian Noble and some of the things he spoke about were exactly the way I was thinking. It just seemed the perfect move. I was really happy and excited about what he was talking about with Bradford. They felt like a friendly club and one that had a plan over the next three, four or five years. They weren't just looking at the next season and I wanted to be part of that plan.

Funnily enough, given the April Fool's joke, Warrington talked to me at the last minute. They came up with a reasonably big offer and it was quite a bit more money than I would have been on at Bradford, but I felt that Bulls had the opportunity to be a more dominant force in Super League and that was more important to me.

I have a lot of respect for Paul Cullen, the coach of Warrington, so the offer did make me think, but in the end I went for Bradford. I'd been under enough pressure to deliver in Wales and I thought if I went back to Leeds or Warrington, it would be there again. Everyone would expect the trophies to roll in and for me to pick up exactly where I left off.

Not everyone agreed with my move. I was surprised to receive some criticism from Jonathan Davies, who, I believe unfairly, suggested I had handled the move badly. I have a lot of respect for Jonathan, so I wouldn't fall out with him over something like this but I was a little bit disappointed with his comments because he didn't have all the facts, although if he'd wanted them all he needed to do was give me a ring.

In his column for BBC online Jonathan said:

> Whether Iestyn Harris's move to the Bradford Bulls will be a good one remains to be seen, but I don't think he's handled it very well in going back. With the contract that he had in rugby union there was always a backdoor exit to it. If things didn't work out there was an escape for him – and maybe he did use that as a slight excuse to go back. He could have been more courteous with Leeds Rhinos, although it's difficult to see where his options were with the salary cap. The contract situation concerning his return to league is so complex that I don't think anyone knows what is happening – including Iestyn.

He went on to say that Leeds Rhinos chief executive Gary Hetherington saw me as their star man before I left and would certainly have wanted first call on me if I returned to rugby league: 'Bradford are a good club and maybe they're looking at him to play stand-off, because they haven't really recovered the great form they showed when Henry Paul was playing six for them.'

He then addressed the issue of my playing union with Wales:

> I don't think Iestyn's applied himself as well as he could have, but I also don't think that those around him have helped. He was rushed into the Wales team purely for financial motives when he wasn't ready for Test rugby. He should have played at inside-centre rather than fly-half from the start, whereas we've only seen him at 12 for one season. It's a blow for Wales because he's a very talented individual and we haven't seen the best of him, and the more talented players we have the better we will do at regional and international level.

Jonathan suggested I might have burnt my bridges with rugby union but I certainly didn't see it that way. It was strange, as he said things that were completely untrue, so I rang him up. He assured me that it wasn't said in a malicious way but should be taken with a pinch of salt, so I accepted that. I have been friends with Jonathan for a long time and now he is in the media things are often taken out of context.

Fortunately, while Jonathan didn't seem to think too much of my decision, it went down very well at Bradford and it meant a lot to me to get the immediate backing of Bulls skipper Robbie Paul. Robbie has been a rival, and a friend, for many years and I have great respect for him as a world-class rugby league player. He said, 'I'm delighted that Bradford have been able to bring Iestyn Harris on board. It really is a massive boost for the club. He's a world-class talent, a player who makes things happen in attack.

But before we go overboard about Iestyn, we must all take a step back and give the guy time to adjust to rugby league. He's been playing union now for three years and is going to need some time to get back into the swing of things.

'We can't heap too much pressure on him.'

Apart from the legal problems, everything else went smoothly. I agreed terms pretty quickly and they wanted me to come on board as soon as possible, so once I got over my knee injury it was back to work.

I don't regret going back and I regret nothing of what I did in rugby union. I played in the Six Nations and a World Cup, made some fantastic friends and enjoyed every minute of it. I have no doubt that I am also a better rugby player for my time in Wales. It was a big wrench for me and Becky to leave. We had made some great friends there and when we did finally settle in our new house up north, we were a bit lost for the first few weeks.

We still keep in touch with those friends in Cardiff and we make it down or they come up whenever we can fit it in. I still have lots of friends in the Cardiff team, like Rhys Williams, Jamie Robinson, Martyn Williams and Tom Shanklin. Friendships I hope I will keep for the rest of my life.

TWO

BACK TO MY ROOTS

My journey to Wales had started back in 1946, many, many years before I was born, when a young rugby union player from south Wales, Norman Harris, decided, like so many young Welshmen before and after him, to go 'north' and play rugby league, the professional game.

My grandfather, who played for Ebbw Vale before moving on to Newbridge, was a centre and won wartime caps for Wales, partnering the father of the future Lions captain John Dawes. He signed for Oldham, later plying his trade at Leigh, before becoming player-coach at Rochdale Hornets. Norman's son Paul, my father, was three when the family moved to Oldham and he ended up playing amateur rugby league for local club Saddleworth Rangers.

I was born on 26 June 1976 in Oldham but being called Iestyn was to prove a bit of a problem in a Lancashire town. In my first day at secondary school, everyone was in the hall and I was sat at the back. They began to read the names out to tell you which class you'd be in and the teacher got stuck, saying, 'I can't pronounce this.' I was cringing at the back because I knew it could only be my name!

I think the headmaster called me 'Einstein', so I was Einstein during my first year at school. That's why, when my daughter was born, I picked a Welsh name that was easy to pronounce.

As my dad played for Saddleworth, it was only natural for me to go along and watch him, which I remember doing from the age of around eight. There was no rugby league played at my junior school, Rushcroft, but my dad took me along to Saddleworth to 'have a look'. I remember my mum said I wouldn't like it, as it was too rough (I'm sure all mums say that), but I loved it.

At eight years of age, I was into every sport – football, cricket, athletics, you name it – so I jumped at the chance of trying this new sport, especially as it was one my dad played. I don't think it was his way of getting me into rugby league because he didn't even know that the Under-9s would be playing that day.

Looking back, I suppose it was even better because I found, or rather bumped into, the sport of rugby league without anyone pushing me into it. You hear of so many kids who are taken along to play sport by well-meaning parents and they are often turned off because their parents are so pushy. That certainly wasn't the case with my mum and dad. I discovered the game on my own, although when I started playing, my dad couldn't have been more supportive.

The Under-9s trained on Wednesdays and played on Sundays and I don't think my dad missed one session; he always drove me the 25 minutes from home to Saddleworth. His support was crucial but the guy who really kept me interested was Dennis Maders, the coach of the Under-9s at the time. His son played in the side and, as often happens in rugby clubs, Dennis ended up coaching us through the age groups from Under-9s to Under-14s. They used to have an all-weather pitch at Saddleworth and that's where I started out. Nowadays, youngsters at Under-9s or Under-10s would probably play tag but in those days it was full contact right from the start.

At that age, if you're any good, they stick you in the middle; if you're not, they stick you out wide, so for the first two or three years I was stuck on the wing, where you might make two or three tackles in a game and touch the ball a couple of times.

I'd like to say I made a glorious start to my rugby league career and that my future success was all down to natural talent but the reality was somewhat different. I don't think we won a game for years. Dennis preached the simple gospel of going out and enjoying yourself; it wasn't about winning and losing.

As an eight year old, I wasn't too bothered about being stuck on the wing, I just loved to play; but as I progressed through the age groups, I got closer and closer to the action.

In the first year, it was just friendlies but as the team stayed together they entered us into a league. At that time, we always seemed to have around 13 players. We rarely had any subs and almost always lost, but what we did have was a great spirit. The same guys week in week out were giving their all for their mates.

The defeats didn't dishearten me, mainly because Dennis was so good with the training. He used to do all the fundamentals but explained them in such an entertaining way that it was a pleasure to be in the team. I think too many coaches of youngsters make the mistake of taking their sport too seriously; Dennis used to treat it as a bit of fun and never put too much pressure on us to win.

However, I do remember one time when it seemed that even Dennis was despairing of our defence and employed Ellery Hanley (or so we thought) to help us. Unbeknown to us, Dennis asked my dad to make a tackle bag to look like Ellery Hanley. At the time, Dad worked in the Scenery Department at Granada TV and duly obliged.

Dennis announced to us that at our next indoor gym session at Clarksfield School the great Ellery Hanley would be attending to show us how to tackle since we had been losing quite heavily recently. Everybody was very excited, as Ellery was one of the best players in the world at the time.

When the session arrived, we were surprised to see a lot of

parents in the gym. Word had obviously got around that the great man was coming and there were one or two autograph books lying around. We all sat cross-legged as Dennis got ready to introduce the great man. 'And now let's welcome all the way from Wigan, Ellery Hanley,' said Dennis. At this point, my dad, who was hiding outside, came in carrying this six-foot home-made tackle bag resplendent in full rugby kit and sporting Ellery's face.

You could have heard a pin drop and then the laughter started! I don't know who was more surprised, the boys or the parents, but we all proceeded to knock hell out of that tackle bag for the next hour or so – great stuff. That was typical Dennis!

Another great example of the way he inspired us youngsters with laughter was our end-of-season treat in the Under-10s. He announced that we would be going on a weekend camp to 'LLAREGGUB', so when all the boys met at the clubhouse one Saturday morning, everyone was excited about what we thought would be a trip to Wales. Some of the dads were there to provide the transport, so we piled into the cars with our tents and picnics and off we went.

'Here we are,' exclaimed Dennis after about three-quarters of a mile, as we pulled up to a gated field. We were surprised as we were expecting a long journey. 'Here we are,' he said again, 'I promised you "LLAREGGUB".' (Spell the word backwards to reveal what he'd really promised.) We all piled out laughing and had a great time camping out – all of us, that is, except our prop-forward Simon Cuthill. Simon lived on the farm adjacent to our camp. He was devastated, poor lad, but he came round in the end!

The secondary school I'd moved to, Royton and Crompton, had no rugby league tradition but it wasn't really a problem because of what we had at Saddleworth.

I say there was no rugby league at Royton and Crompton but that isn't strictly true. I remember that there was another player from Saddleworth Rangers there, so we set up a team. However, we lost our first game 84–0, so they decided they weren't going to bother again, which I suppose is hardly surprising. I never really missed it at school because I did so many other sports.

All the parents were heavily involved at Saddleworth and after a while my dad became assistant coach of the side. It was difficult to get referees, so he even took on that role on a number of occasions. My mum, Sandra, has always been involved in rugby, especially as my dad had always played. She and my sister, Rhiain, who is four years older than me, used to come down and help out. They'd come to the games and do the soup for us. I always thought it was great having my family involved in the club in that way and their support has remained strong throughout my career.

It wasn't until I was in the Under-14s that I scored my first try. I was hooker at the time and must have been one of the only players in the team not to have scored. A few of my teammates were trying to create try-scoring positions for me and in the end I made it, a dive over from a yard, against Widnes Tigers, a day I'll never forget.

As I made my way through the age groups at Saddleworth I went from wing to hooker and on to prop and second row. It was only in my last year as an amateur, at 16, that I moved to stand-off. There were a number of factors that contributed to my transformation from a below-average player to one who could go on and become a professional in such a short space of time. I think I always had the fundamentals, thanks to Dennis, I just needed the size. Fortunately I had a growth spurt at just the right time.

Many who played under Dennis went on to play at quite a high level as amateurs. They all got a really good understanding of the game and if you have that at a young age it gives you the chance to progress. Dennis is still around, although I don't see him as much any more. I hope he has taken a lot of pride in my career and I know Saddleworth's youth set-up is still prospering.

Apart from Dennis and my dad, I also had a lot of other help along the way. I remember one guy who really did make a big difference to my development, former Huddersfield player Jimmy

Russell. Jimmy did a lot of sprint coaching with me. From the age of 12 to around 17 I used to work with him twice a week and he never charged me a penny.

Jimmy was a great guy and would take me down to the sprint track in Oldham, which is now a B&Q store. He wasn't attached to Oldham or any other club but used to play with my dad and was a great mate of his. I don't see him as much now but I owe him a big debt. He started the sessions with just me and then a couple of other players came along, so the number in the group would rise and fall. We used to go every Tuesday and Thursday, either side of my training sessions with Dennis at Saddleworth, and there were very few sessions that I missed. You take it for granted at the time but, looking back, his dedication was incredible. He had no reason to do it but he was still there come rain or shine.

I'm not sure from where I got the drive to want to improve at that age but encouragement from my parents was crucial. My dad was brilliant with me in my early years. He had the knack of pushing the right buttons, but not pushing them too hard. I also have to give him the credit for my sidestep. When I was young, we had a caravan and I was always taking my dad on, one-on-one, around the caravan, trying to beat him with my footwork. That lasted from when I was six up until thirteen or fourteen. Some people have suggested my sidestep was a natural attribute but my dad and I know how much work went into it around that caravan. Not one moment was wasted and even on our summer holidays I'd take a ball and put in time, trying to be a better player.

Dad always took me to football or cricket training and took an interest in anything I did. I hope he knows how much I owe him for that. Whatever I decided to do, inside or outside sport, he would have backed me all the way. When I played Academy rugby league, he used to drive me up to Warrington for every session and he never grumbled.

Obviously, I dreamed of making it as a professional player but that was never my goal in my teenage years. Just becoming as good as I could be was my objective and I take a great deal of pride in how my hard work has paid off. I'm proof that no matter how slowly you progress at first, if you work hard you can achieve your goals.

Dennis Maders left Saddleworth when I was about 13 or 14 and the team split up, so I moved to Oldham St Annes, one of the best amateur sides in the town. From there, I got into the Oldham town team, which I don't think I would have done from Saddleworth. There's always a club that's looked on more favourably for the town team and St Annes was that club.

The Deakin family were heavily involved in the club. Peter became marketing manager at the Bradford Bulls, was chief executive at Warrington and went on to work for Saracens, while his brother Steve is coaching the new French club, Les Catalans, who will be in Super League in 2006. My dad had also played for St Annes and I knew a lot of people there. I only played for one season but I really enjoyed it.

As I was developing as a player, I got the chance to represent English Schools. I remember reading in Clive Woodward's book *Winning* that while studying at a Welsh school, he had trials for Welsh Schools. It appears he was made to feel unwelcome but I certainly can't say the same of my time with English Schools. I had an English accent but my name signified I was Welsh; however, the question of my Welsh roots never really came up. There was no rugby league in Wales at that time, so there wasn't an option for me to play representative rugby there. For me, it was the highest honour but that didn't mean I had any intention of playing international rugby for England.

We had Lancashire trials, then Lancashire against Yorkshire and from there 22 players were picked to go to France with the English Schools Under-15s for two Tests. I was picked at second row and that was the first time I thought I might be able to make my mark in this sport. We had some good players, including John McAtee, Jon Roper and Marcus Vassilakopoulos.

I was the only one from Oldham to make the squad and it was

significant because it meant that I had, in one selection, leapt over all those players who had been classed above me in the last few years. That selection was a huge fillip for my career.

It could have led me to think I was better than I was but luckily it made me realise how much I enjoyed the sport and how, with a lot of hard work, I could make a professional career out of it. It gave me a taste of representative rugby and made me realise I wanted a lot more of it.

After that, I played for the Oldham town team at Under-16s and that led me to signing for Warrington. During one game at Watersheddings, the old home of Oldham rugby league club, Jim Reader, who was chief scout with Warrington at the time, came and sat next to my dad. I don't know whether that was intentional or not but he started talking to him about me.

I was playing loose forward at the time. Peter Tunks was the Oldham coach and Iain McCorquodale, who was deputy head at my school North Chadderton, was involved at the club as well. It was exciting because I wanted to play professionally but wondered if I would be good enough. I was told by Peter that I was never going to be big enough to be a forward and he didn't think I was fast enough to be a back. But he thought I was OK and said they would be willing to offer me a contract.

However, Warrington were also offering me terms. Oldham offered more money than Warrington but they didn't have an academy, which Warrington did. Oldham wanted me to carry on playing at St Annes and stay in the amateur game before going into the first team when I was ready.

I looked at the pros and cons and thought if I stay in the amateur game it's going to be really tough to step up into the professional game. I remember a guy called Richard Badby, a sensational player who had everything you could possibly ask for. He signed for Oldham in 1992, started playing for St Annes and never came out of the amateur ranks. If you stay at amateur level, it's nigh on impossible to get out of it and I'm sure if he had chosen a different club he'd have made it.

People often ask what happened to Oldham rugby league club. In 1996, they were in Super League but are now at the bottom end of National One. You can put it down to that one thing, youth – they never bothered enough with the youngsters.

I felt Warrington was the better option and, looking back, it was a really good decision. They were perfect for me. Brian Johnson, the coach, and his assistant, Clive Griffiths, really believed in youth and I'm sure that many of those who were there at the time, like Paul Sculthorpe and Mike Wainwright, would say exactly the same.

I signed amateur forms with Warrington when I was 15, which committed me to signing for them professionally at 17. It was the norm at the time and my father signed on my behalf.

I had really high hopes of turning professional, so I was determined that I would enjoy my last year as an amateur. I played for Seddon Atkinson Under-18s, who were in the North West Counties league. All my friends were playing for them and it was really competitive. I used to train at Warrington on Tuesdays and Thursdays and play for them on Saturdays. On Wednesdays I'd train with Seddon Atkinson and play for them on Sundays.

Warrington couldn't say too much about me playing amateur rugby league at the same time as playing for them because I was only 16 and wasn't a professional yet.

I was really glad I did because it was probably the most enjoyable season I had in the amateur ranks. I loved it and I reckoned that if I could cope with that workload then it would stand me in good stead in future years.

Five or six of the Warrington Under-19 side I played for during the 1992–93 season had the same contracts as I did and the rest were hoping to do enough to get professional contracts. Of course, signing at 15 didn't mean you were guaranteed a five-year professional contract at 17 and it was made very clear to me how much work would have to be done in those two years. But the prospect of that contract at 17 acted as a massive incentive for me. I knew that if I worked hard and improved, there was a professional career waiting for me at Warrington.

Contracts like that, which were effectively for seven years and cover the transition from being an amateur to a professional player, can breed complacency but I never felt like that. I knew I had a lot more work to do and my father always told me that I was at the bottom of the ladder and not the top. You see players who relax and say, 'That's me for seven years.' Those sort of players have never gone on to have a successful career and usually find themselves playing in the lower leagues or even going back to the amateur ranks.

Lots of players have natural ability but it's those who are prepared to work hard that tend to succeed. Many who get regional or national honours in their early teens don't go on to make it. I'm not sure why but I think that in a lot of instances those who prosper early on find it easy and feel they don't have to work. That certainly wasn't the case with me. I've always enjoyed training and love getting stuck in.

Take someone like Lawrence Dallaglio, for example. He is one of the best players I've ever seen, in either union or league. His asset is his size and his strength but I wouldn't say he was one of the most naturally talented rugby players I've ever seen. Crucially, however, Lawrence, and many others like him, have worked hard and made the absolute most of what they do have.

It is also the case with Jonny Wilkinson. At the end of the 2003 Rugby World Cup, Jonny was perhaps the best rugby union player in the world. I'm not sure if you'll find a more dedicated player than him. His hours of practising are legendary and he shows what you can achieve if you set your mind to it. There are so many players like that. The ones who work the hardest usually have the most success.

My burgeoning rugby career was to have an effect on my education. I had left Royton and Crompton secondary school at 14 to go to North Chadderton. I wanted to go into the sixth form and do A levels but Royton and Crompton didn't have a sixth form and North Chadderton did. If you went there, you got into their sixth form automatically whereas if you didn't you had to apply.

I always struggled academically. I had private lessons to get me through some of my exams and I eventually got seven GCSEs, but I wouldn't class myself as a fast learner, I had to work at it.

In my first year in the sixth form, I was doing English Literature, English Language, Design Technology and Sociology. Although I found it hard to keep up with them, I was enjoying it because I had such a good circle of friends. Every dinner and every break time we used to play football and even now I keep in contact with 12 or 13 of my friends from school. So I have great memories from that period of my life.

As far as career options were concerned, if I didn't make it as a professional player I wanted to go into the police or be a social worker. Then Warrington offered me a full-time contract, so I ended up not taking my A levels. It was a big decision to go full time with rugby but I think it was the right one, things turned out OK.

I enjoyed some success in that talented Warrington Under-19s side. Coming up through amateur rugby league, you were all of a similar frame and size but in my first professional season I experienced a big step up in the physical side of the game. It was the first time I'd really felt what a physical sport rugby league was. All of a sudden, you were coming up against players who'd done weights longer than you and were just physically bigger and stronger. It made me realise how much physical work I had to do to catch up.

I was one of two or three sixteen year olds in our team and I was lucky in that Warrington had a fantastic youth system. They really looked after that Under-19 side and it is one of the main reasons I went on to have success in both league and union. It is so important, in any sport, to get a good grounding and Warrington made sure we did.

Today everyone talks about their youth policy but back in the early 1990s it wasn't like that at every club. However, Brian

Johnson, the head coach at Warrington, put a lot of time and effort into the youth side. He was way ahead of his time in this respect.

You have to remember it was a completely different sport from the one we have today. Before the advent of Super League in 1996, most rugby league players were semi-professional. Warrington weren't overburdened with financial backers at that time and Brian and his assistant coach Clive Griffiths realised that the youth players would have to be the first-teamers of tomorrow, so they made sure the fundamentals were put in place early.

Once a fortnight, on a Monday night, he insisted that the whole club trained together, from us wide-eyed teenagers in the youth set-up to the first-team players who'd been around for decades. And you can imagine, the opportunity to train with the first team acted as a real inspiration for us in the Under-19s. There I was, a 16 year old playing amateur rugby league one day and then training with Jonathan Davies the next! I think there were around 50 to 55 of us in those sessions and we got a taste of first-team action. It made all of us train a little harder so we could make the grade ourselves.

Brian ensured that the Under-19s weren't patronised on those Monday nights. We did a lot of physical stuff and the message to us youngsters was clear – 'If you aren't physical enough you won't make it.' The coaches explained that we had a lot of work to do and it showed me how far I had to go.

It was a great experience. Even those players who didn't make it to the highest level could look back on those Monday night sessions with fond memories. The club captain at the time was Greg Mackey and he was someone else who was great with the youngsters. I think that came down from Brian and Clive.

In a way it sounds obvious and you would think that every club would employ some of those methods today but there are still some, in league and union, who pay little more than lip service to their youth policy.

It you wanted to do extra work on the back of your sessions you could call the other coaches, including those who worked on conditioning. I was a pretty late starter on the weights, and hadn't done any until I was 16. Today, that would be considered very late but I was lucky that I went on the right programme, one that could be supervised by a professional club with professional coaches.

We were all great friends in that Warrington Under-19 team and we had an excellent coach in Chris Middlehurst. Although we were part of a professional club I always remember Chris telling us that we were his boys and that was important. Chris wasn't the most technical of coaches but he gave us something more. Boys of 16, 17, 18 and 19 have a lot of stuff going through their heads and a lot of things on their plate, so having Chris with us was just what we needed, he always looked after us.

I remember him saying he wouldn't let us move up to the A team, which was the next level up, until we were ready. Chris kept a real fatherly eye on the whole side. At the time, it was a little frustrating as some of us wanted to move up but Chris thought we weren't ready and we knew in our heart of hearts that he was right, he was acting in our best interests.

When you're a teenager and have a chance of playing senior rugby you want to grab it in case it never comes around again. Clive was coaching the A team at the time and I know he was keen for some of the Under-19 side to move up and get some A team experience. I had the offer of a couple of A team games right at the end of the year but Chris wouldn't allow it.

Chris's policy was good for another reason: it meant we were all focused on our team, and as a result we had a really good year together. Colin Hodgkinson was my captain in that last season at Under-19. He was one of the players who'd played some first-team rugby and then come back to the Academy. There were others in that side, like Mike Wainwright and Jon Roper, who went on to play for Warrington's first team.

I was playing loose forward then and it was also my first year as a goalkicker. I didn't start goalkicking until a certain Dave

Alred, the current England rugby union kicking coach, came to Warrington to hold a clinic. All of us were asked if we fancied having a go at goalkicking. Even though I was a prop at the time, I stuck up my hand and went with four or five others to have some coaching from Dave. I'm sure at the time Dave never imagined that a decade later I'd be travelling to Twickenham, with the Wales team, to take on his England side. Considering the amount of kicking coaching he's done, he must be forever running into former pupils.

The 1992–93 season was a great one for that Warrington Under-19 side. Hull were our big rivals; they also had a good youth set-up and we had some epic encounters. I think we played them two or three times that season and even in that age group they were very physical encounters as they had a number of 18 and 19 year olds in their team.

They were the better side throughout the year but we had the chance to make amends when we met them in the Academy Challenge Cup final at the end of the season. At that time, the Premiership finals were held at Old Trafford in May and the Academy game was played as a curtain raiser to that match.

As a Manchester United fan, it was a huge thrill for me to run out at the Theatre of Dreams. I had gone to Old Trafford to watch Manchester United play at the start of the 1990s but as I was playing so much rugby league I wasn't able to go and see them as much as I would have liked. To play there was very special, something I'd dreamed about.

There were almost 40,000 in for the main game but sadly there were hardly any in for our match, which was a little disappointing. At the start the terraces were empty but by the end I suppose there were five to ten thousand in. Still, it didn't spoil a great day.

I think our fantastic team spirit was a big factor on the day and we went on to win 19–12. I couldn't manage a try but I kicked some goals. It was my first trophy, my first taste of success and something I will never forget.

I signed professional terms with Warrington in June 1993, as soon as I turned 17. I think I got a £7,000 signing on fee and they gave me an old clapped-out Nissan which had gone once round the clock. Everything was bonus-related, so if you played five first-team games they'd give you so much, ten first-team games you'd get so much, and so on.

Once you broke into that first team and had a bit of success, they renegotiated pretty quickly. At the time Warrington were very fair with the younger players, renegotiating their contracts early on. They could have left them on just bonuses for the five years, but they didn't.

I must admit, in that first season as a professional with Warrington, I was in something of a whirlwind. I moved up to the A team, which was coached by Clive Griffiths, a former Wales rugby union international full-back who had signed for St Helens before moving on to Salford and then getting into coaching. He has been so supportive of me throughout my career and I'm sure Clive put in a few good words for me with Brian Johnson. He helped me with my kicking and kept popping up throughout my league career. In fact, he was still on the scene in 2005 as the Wales defence coach when they won the Grand Slam.

I think Clive took a shine to me as a young Welsh player coming through. There was quite a big Welsh contingent at Warrington at the time. Alongside Clive and Jonathan were Allan Bateman, Kevin Ellis and Rowland Phillips.

Clive asked me to play for the Welsh Students that season and he had even called me into the Wales squad when they were taking on New Zealand at the Vetch Field in Swansea on 3 October. I didn't play but it was great experience, particularly as I had still to make my first-team debut for Warrington.

Soon after that I was chosen for the Lancashire Academy team to play the Junior Kiwis at St Helens. It was the first time I came up against a young New Zealander called Henry Paul. We came so close to beating them, eventually losing to a last-minute goal from Henry, who was tour captain, which gave them a 16–14 victory.

My performance for the Lancashire Academy meant it wouldn't be the last time I'd see those Junior Kiwis on that tour. I was fortunate enough to be brought into Great Britain's Academy side to play them at Wembley, a warm-up game before the Great Britain v. New Zealand international on 16 October.

That trip to Wembley was the latest stop in an incredible journey I was on in 1993. I remember we had been written off before going into that game but there was a growing belief that we were developing into an impressive generation of Great Britain rugby league players. The academy system meant that this Under-19 side had a far better chance of succeeding than many before. We weren't being thrown together, we were in a structure and I was starting to get used to playing with players from other clubs.

John Kear, who was then the Rugby Football League's Academy executive, was another great support for me. He even used me as an example of how well the Academy system was developing.

We put up an incredibly good performance at Wembley, eventually losing 30–22, but we were proud of the way we came back from 22–8 down. There was a real backbone in that Great Britain side – we didn't know when we were beaten.

The Kiwis were a tough physical group that included Joe Vagana, a fearsome prop with whom I later teamed up at Bradford. But Henry Paul was the star of the side and little did I know how many times he would cross my path in the ensuing years.

What a gifted player Henry was! They had talented players throughout their squad and arrived in Great Britain with an air of invincibility around them. We did reasonably well against them and, looking back, we could take a lot from that series.

Wembley was a very special day for me, not just because of running out onto that famous turf but also because of the 60-yard try I scored. In the process I went around Henry so it was a great memory for me, even though I was still on the wing.

However, Henry had the final say, rounding off a marvellous

personal performance with the match-clinching try, his second, right at the death. He also kicked the conversion to take his points tally for the game to sixteen as the Junior Kiwis made it seven wins out of seven on their British tour.

Not long after that game at Wembley, I was lining up to take them on again, this time as part of Great Britain's Under-19 side. We played at Wigan and managed to inflict on them the only defeat of their tour. And if that wasn't enough, on 26 October, I took the field against the full New Zealand side for the Great Britain Under-21s, making my debut for another new team under the captaincy of Andy Farrell.

To be honest, I was still dreaming as it rounded off a couple of amazing months for me. At the start of September very few people had heard of Iestyn Harris and now it was nearly the end of October and I was on my way to Workington to take on New Zealand.

Unfortunately, the game didn't go too well. We went 12–6 ahead after I managed to kick conversions to tries from Hull's Rob Danby and Wigan's Farrell but New Zealand hit back and led 13–12 at half-time. However, in the second half they pulled away from us and in the end we just couldn't match them physically. It was a talented team which included future stars like Barrie Jon Mather and Mick Cassidy.

That was my first match in the same side as Andy Farrell, who followed me from league into union. At the time Andy, who is a year older than me, was a rising star. He was a big, strong second rower. Even at that early age, he seemed to have everything and he's gone on to fulfil that early promise.

In many ways it was amazing that newspapers the next day referred to me as 'Warrington's Iestyn Harris', despite the fact that I still hadn't played for the first team! Everything was flowing so well for me in my career at the time and it was a case of having to pinch myself just to make sure I wasn't dreaming.

I was picking up man of the match awards, playing well for Great Britain Academy, the Under-21s and I even got picked to go on the Great Britain Academy tour at the end of the year. But I was still frustrated because each time I was being picked on the wing, although I was playing full-back for the Warrington A team.

John Kear was great, giving us guys the opportunity to play on some great pitches and to test ourselves against some great players. It was an excellent system. I had a joke with John some years later about him sticking me on the wing in that season and again on the summer tour that followed and he accepted they should have moved me in sooner.

I spoke to Brian Johnson at the time and he said, 'Just be patient, it will come, you're only 17. We're bringing you on the right way and eventually you will move in from the wing.' But rather than reassuring me that frustrated me even more!

Obviously at that age you just want to play but hopefully it showed my drive. The likes of Anthony Sullivan, Alan Hunte and Martin Offiah were the world-class wings at that time and they were clocking nearly 10 seconds for the 100 metres. I was never going to get to that pace. I knew wing was never going to work for me and that I needed to move in to take my career to the next level. For the time being, I had to grin and bear it although, three days after that game against New Zealand at Workington, I achieved another milestone when I made my senior debut for Warrington.

From an early age, all I wanted to do was to play rugby at the highest level, so when I ran out for Warrington on 29 October 1993 against Leigh in the Stones Bitter Championship it was more than a dream come true. It was all I had ever worked for.

I had always imagined what it would be like to run out for a professional club and when I did get my chance, it was extra special.

Although I'd been picked on the wing, I'd be taking over the goalkicking duties. And I wouldn't be taking those duties over from just anyone, but from a man whom I'd stood and watched in awe down the years, playing union and league at the highest level, Jonathan Davies.

I was still at school studying for my A levels at North Chadderton College when I made my first-team debut. I knew earlier in the week that Jonathan was doubtful but I didn't think for one moment it would be me who'd come in. Looking back, as I was the Warrington A team kicker, it should have been obvious but I have never taken any selection for granted.

I had trained with the first team on the Monday and they had told me Jonathan was injured. Brian Johnson said, 'Come in and train with us this week, but Jonathan could still be fit for Friday.' As you can imagine it was one of the longest weeks of my life waiting to see if I was in at last.

I think Jonathan pulled out on the Wednesday, and it was confirmed almost immediately that I would play. Brian Johnson came and told me and he was very good, boosting my confidence and explaining the faith he had in me. I had been playing full-back for the A team and I'm not sure if Brian knew it would be the first game of my senior life on the wing. If he didn't know I certainly wasn't going to tell him.

I remember on the Thursday, at the last training session before the match, Brian made everyone line up and he handed me the ball in front of the whole first team. He then said, 'Right, it's the last minute on Saturday. We are one point down and we have a kick on the 30-metre line to win the match. Kick it over.' So I trotted off in front of the whole squad and kicked the goal. Everyone went mad, celebrating as if we had won the cup. They certainly made me feel very welcome. Brian particularly was a great man-manager and his help meant so much to me.

Brian had one piece of psychology which he worked on me just as we were getting ready to face Leigh. We were in the dressing-room before the game and I was sitting there as nervous as you can imagine. He came up to me and said, 'Do you know what I want you to do differently in this game than any other game you have played before?' I was immediately stumped and blurted out, 'I don't know.' He replied, 'Nothing, I don't want you to do anything differently. Do exactly what you have done in other games. Now go out there and enjoy it!' As you can imagine, it settled me down and sent me out full of confidence.

My nerves were also helped by the fact that the game was subject to a Harris family pilgrimage. I have never looked for family or friends in a crowd but it was good to know they were there. My mum, my father, my sister, Rhiain, and my granddad came to the game. As it was being televised on Sky, a lot of my friends decided to watch it in the pub or at home but I knew they were all rooting for me. I also remember Clive Griffiths telling me to calm down, relax and enjoy it. I had the backing of the head coach and the assistant coach and that made a lot of difference to a 17-year-old lad from Oldham about to make his professional debut.

That changing-room at Wilderspool was filled with legends. At the time, it was my cup final, the biggest game of my career, so I was nervous and excited at the same time. The rest of the players were probably thinking, 'This is just another game. It's only Leigh and we are expected to win.' They were feeling a lot different to me but everyone tried their best to take some time and calm my nerves. I just remember it as a really good experience.

The fact that it was on Sky was another bonus. I had played on television once before in Warrington's Under-19 Cup final the season before, but this was very different. An amazing experience! Of course I was nervous. Wouldn't you be? I had watched Jonathan on the television all those times, playing for Wales. He was a hero. To be taking his place in a professional rugby league match was simply Boy's Own stuff.

But the nerves disappeared once I ran out there. Once you cross the white line, there's no time for nerves.

I made a break early on. I remember stepping and going through, which really settled me. Hearing the crowd was another new experience – listening to seven or eight thousand people roaring was something very different for the young Iestyn Harris, who had been in a classroom the day before. In the A team we'd get the die-hard six or seven hundred but it was nothing like this.

First-team crowds were different. Many had supported Warrington for decades and had seen players come and go. They had seen the 'flash in the pans' but they gave me a fantastic reception and that helped as well.

I was in something of a whirl at the time. I was still at school, studying for my A levels, so to be thrown into a top-level rugby league match at that stage was a real baptism of fire. I had school in the day, training at night, and then at the end of the week I was playing for one of the top professional rugby league sides.

The teachers were always interested and sometimes I would find them coming over and talking to me about rugby league while the lessons were going on. Friends are friends and I didn't find them treating me any differently just because I was playing for Warrington. For me, of course, it wasn't unusual. I was just getting on with my studies – nothing could have been more natural. But I was thrilled to be getting the chance to play professional rugby league.

We beat Leigh 24–6 and I managed to kick four of six goal attempts. I remember all those six kicks as if they had happened yesterday.

My first kick gave us the lead but it only went over after hitting the post. I was hoping that the first penalty, if it came, would be straightforward and this one was so I didn't have much difficulty. I remember Leigh's Andy Collier was penalised when he tackled Kelly Shelford.

The next day in *The Independent* newspaper Dave Hadfield described that first successful kick as 'a simple penalty'. At the time, it was anything but a simple penalty, although I know what Dave meant. It was just outside the 22 and to the side of the posts. My memory is of scuffing it and then holding my breath as it hit the post and struggled over. It was reasonably early on in the game after they had scored first so it was good to get one over no matter how scrappily.

Leigh were a very physical side and I knew that as a 17-year-old goalkicker, in my first match, I had a target on my back. I remember getting a crack around the head in the first few minutes but I knew it was coming.

Although Leigh had lost eight on the trot coming into that match they were powerful in defence and it took us ages to break them down. When we did, we scored a few tries and although I didn't touch down myself, I'd like to think I did enough to make myself useful on the field. It was a great day, one I will never forget.

I suppose there was less pressure on me as I was only in the team because Jonathan was injured. I was under no illusions about this being a full-time position for me and perhaps that allowed me to enjoy it more. That win took us to the top of the table alongside Wigan and Bradford.

It was a massive thrill for me and it lived up to all my expectations. After the match the Sky reporter grabbed me for an interview. It was my first – I still have the tape somewhere and I think I said 'superb' about eight times, which I got a lot of stick for afterwards. Every time I walked into a clubhouse, especially Royton Cricket Club where there were loads watching me that night, someone would shout 'superb'. I remember saying hello to all my family and friends as I thought it might be the last interview I would ever do.

I kept my place for the next game, away at Salford, which we won 20–6 and once again I kicked four goals. Tries had been harder to come by but that all changed in the next game at home to Hunslet in the second round of the Regal Trophy, the midseason knockout competition.

My tries were like buses. None came along for a while and then it was a case of three at once. Both Lee Penny and myself scored hat-tricks in the 58–16 win. I don't remember any pressure coming from the team or the coaches but it's obviously good to get that first try under your belt and for two more to follow in the same game made it extra special. I did feel that it lifted some of the pressure and made me even more accepted around the first team.

We scored 16 points in the first 11 minutes to put the game beyond Hunslet's reach. I scored one long-distance try and another two from short range. Having Jonathan back in the team for that match made a huge difference and I remember him scoring a great solo try.

You treat your first match as if it could be your last but once you play in two or three you start to feel more comfortable. However, just as I was getting used to it, my run in the first team came to an end. I was left out for the match against Castleford in favour of Chris Rudd. Brian said he didn't want to rush me but as a 17 year old all I wanted to do was play rugby, so it was a big disappointment. Looking back, I can see exactly what he was getting at, but at the time it was hard to accept, especially as I'd scored a hat-trick in the last game. I was still there to support the boys, though, and we won 20–10, which was extra special as it took us to the top of the First Division for the first time in four years.

Early in December I played for Great Britain Under-21s against France Under-21s at Wilderspool. The young Lions had lost to France at Wigan in 1991, 16–6, so we knew this could be a tough encounter. The side had a good record against France but with Andy Farrell injured the contest was evened up a little more. The match turned out to be one of my most memorable as I scored a try and kicked four goals in our 28–16 victory.

In that first year of professional rugby, every time Jonathan was either injured or away on international duty I was called up to the first team, as they had no other kicker. I found myself in a bizarre situation. I cheered Jonathan on to get GB caps but I found myself jumping up when he got a dead leg or something similar. It's probably the wrong thing to do but at that age you just want to get in there!

In that season I was turning out for the A team on Thursday night and then the first team, when they needed me, on the weekend. All in all I played ten times for the first team in that season. Brian was very keen to ease me in gently and it definitely worked.

It was quite unusual at the time to go from a season in the Under-19s, when I was still playing amateur rugby league, to my debut as a professional for the first team, but like most teenagers I didn't really think about it that way. I just took on every challenge as it came along. Everything went better than I could have hoped in that first season. The goals were going over and I believed I was getting more and more involved in the games, and most crucially of all, Warrington were winning.

In fact, at the end of the season Warrington were one of three clubs, Wigan and Bradford were the others, to finish on the same number of points, 46. It was the first time this had ever happened but the title went to Wigan who had a superior points difference. Warrington had to be content with third place.

But my incredible first season as a professional wasn't over. I now went on a tough tour to Australia, with the Great Britain Under-19s Academy. It was such a thrill to be selected for that trip but I hadn't realised how hard it would be. It was a tour where the costs were cut to the bare minimum. John Kear was the only coach and we ended up staying in Salvation Army hostels most of the time. I learned so much from that tour. I think you have to go through tough times to learn the hard lessons.

My mother and father came out on that tour so it was great to see them and get away from things by meeting them for a coffee or a meal. I was still only 17 and although you feel like you are grown up, you clearly still need the comfort of your parents.

Jeanette Smith, our physio, was a real heroine on that trip. She worked overtime and took really good care of us.

Nobody would have picked me out as a future professional player when I started my rugby league career as a wing in the Under-9s, and as a wing with no great ability either! But if there has been a key to my success, it has been hard work. I knew from an early age that I wasn't going to make it on natural talent alone, despite what both my father and grandfather had passed down to me. But I had a work ethic, which I am sure I got from them, and it ensured that I went to every training session I was invited to, and a few more besides, working tirelessly on my skills.

That commitment was demonstrated in a very unusual way in that first season as a professional with Warrington. I was playing in the A team, but training on a Tuesday evening with the first team. It was one of my first real sessions with the guys whom I had idolised from the touchline just a few short months before.

There had been a crash on the motorway on that particular Tuesday evening. We had pulled off at Birchwood, which was about four miles from the training ground, but if I knew one thing, it was that I wasn't going to be late for one of my first training sessions with the first team. There was no way I was going to wait and see if the traffic would clear, and as it was bumper to bumper, I decided to run those four miles to the ground.

I remember turning up at training with my white school shirt dripping with sweat. A few of the older guys were looking at me and saying, 'You should have just sat in the car.' How could I do that and risk missing one of my first training sessions with Warrington's first team? Running those four miles was my only option. What else could I do?

When you get older, you know it's acceptable to ring if you are stuck in traffic and to be late now and again. But as a 17-year-old lad, being late just wasn't an option. Looking back, I suppose it shows how determined I was to make it as a professional rugby league player and how I wasn't going to let anything stand in the way of me making it to the top.

In my second season at Warrington, I played most of the first-team games but in my eyes this will always be 'Jonathan's Year'. We believed that 1994–95 could be a big season for us. Wigan got off to an incredible start, equalling the record of 13 consecutive league wins at the start of a season with a 46–0 rout of Oldham. Henry Paul, who had stayed on after the Junior Kiwis tour to play for Wakefield Trinity, subsequently moved to Wigan and was turning in some magnificent performances.

But we were developing into a formidable side, particularly at home.

There were some famous victories in that season and we had a great run in the Regal Trophy competition. We reached the quarter-finals by clawing our way back into a match at Salford where we looked dead and buried. We were 24–10 down at half-time, but came storming back in the second half with 21 unanswered points. There were tries from Greg Mackey, Kelly Shelford and Tukere Barlow, with me kicking four goals and Kelly landing a last-minute drop goal for a 31–24 victory.

We beat Jonathan's former club, Widnes, in the semi-final and he was outstanding. It was an incredible day for him: he landed six goals, including two fabulous drop goals. I was lucky enough to join him on the score sheet that day at Naughton Park, along with Mark Forster, as we moved into the club's seventh Regal Trophy final in 21 years with a 30–4 victory.

After that semi-final, I remember Clive Griffiths was particularly complimentary about my performance. Commenting in the *Daily Mail* at the time he said, 'Iestyn is a perfect example of the benefits that come from playing the game as a kid. He will be the player our development officers in Wales can point to as evidence that you don't need to make your name in union first.'

We were playing Wigan in the final at the McAlpine Stadium, Huddersfield, and I remember we set off from Warrington full of hope, believing it was going to be our day, but a series of events started to go against us.

We had planned to have a police escort to the ground but that didn't materialise, meaning that we were sitting in traffic for what seemed like an eternity. The game was due to kick off at 3 p.m. but we were still stuck on the motorway at 2.15, as there had been a crash, I think. We phoned through to the ground but were told that the game couldn't be delayed because it was being shown live on television. We eventually arrived at 2.45 so we had only 15 minutes to get changed, warm up and get on the pitch.

I suppose it came as no surprise that we were soon a few tries down and in an impossible position. What should have been a great day for the club turned out to be a terrible one. Wigan beat us 40–10, the highest score for any Regal Trophy final – their 6 tries was another best, while Frano Botica set a points-scoring record with 20 from 8 goals and a try. I was at centre that day, up against the mighty Va'aiga Tuigamala. I remember just thinking, 'This guy is humungous.' He must have run over the top of me about six times. Wigan were awesome and had flair everywhere, so it turned into a really long day at the office for us.

That awful day, though, couldn't take all the gloss off our cup run to the final.

Your second season as a professional is often a difficult one because in the first year nobody really knows who you are. They don't know whether you've got a left foot step or a right foot step, but by the next season they have worked you out and will say, 'That's the kid, watch his left foot step or his right foot step.' If you can get through that year, you're well on the way to having a good career in the game.

Take someone like Danny McGuire, the young Leeds stand-off. 2004 was his first major season and he was unstoppable but the next year, while he played well, he was not at the same level because now the opposition knew about him and watched him.

I got the award for Most Improved Player that season and started to learn things off other players. In the previous season, I usually played when Jonathan wasn't available but suddenly I was his winger and was listening to him and watching what he did on the field.

In attack, I'd be looking to see where he was then suddenly he'd be gone. He'd sniffed a break 30 yards away and was under the sticks. You'd say to yourself, 'Why didn't I pick that up?' He could see things unfolding a couple of seconds before other people and I wanted to work out how he did that. I started to look at the game that way and pick things up. To play alongside someone like him at that time was special.

I still felt I was learning. We had Kevin Ellis at six and he was a great player, so I didn't have any qualms about playing on the wing, I was just happy to be in the team.

Jason Robinson signed for Wigan as a scrum-half but when he came in they put him on the wing and he found that to be his best position. It's the easiest way to drag someone through a game. You may have talent and ability but you haven't got the knowledge to play the game at that level. If you put a youngster on the wing, they can almost get away with it through their enthusiasm while they're getting a feel for the game.

I just remember it being a really enjoyable year. I was earning more money than I'd ever earned before, lived with Mum and Dad, had my own car and was having a good time. I could look back on those first two seasons in the Warrington first team with pride. Most importantly it gave me a taste of professional rugby and I wanted more!

THREE

THREE FEATHERS IN MY HEART

Growing up a proud young Welshman in Oldham meant bedtime tales of Edwards, Bennett and John, and daydreams of pulling on that famous red jersey. My father and grandfather ensured the young Iestyn Harris had the three feathers in his heart from day one.

My first memories, from about four or five, were Wales, Wales and just a bit more Wales. The most desperate times came when we played England at football, rugby union or rugby league. We just had to win, it was as simple as that.

As I wasn't a great rugby league player in my early teens, I didn't really believe my time in the Wales jersey would come. Little did I realise that my first call up for Wales would be while I was still at school and it was quite a shock to get the chance so soon. I feel very lucky to have had a career that has included representing Wales at both league and union and of course playing for Great Britain.

I could have played rugby league for England, having been born in Oldham, but to be honest there wasn't even 1 per cent of me that considered turning down the chance to link up with the Wales squad. A lot of players are qualified to play for more than one country and they agonise over which to play for. That wasn't the case with me, not that England had come calling for me at that stage. I gave the call from Wales about two seconds' thinking time. When Clive Griffiths asked me to play, I said yes straight away. Everything felt right and it was exactly what I'd always wanted to do. It was a perfect decision for me and it was an honour to be involved.

Clive had spoken to me at Warrington training to tell me he was going to pull me into the squad. 'I'll bring you in for three or four days to enjoy the experience,' he said.

Then I got a letter of confirmation in the post and it felt really good. Once Clive spoke to me I was straight on the phone to my dad and he was equally thrilled. There was no question of them coming down to watch the game as we all knew I wasn't going to play.

We stayed at the International Hotel in Cardiff and Clive, cleverly, made me share with Peter Williams, the Salford centre who used to play rugby union for Orrell and won four caps for England in 1987. He was 34 or 35 at the time, right at the end of his career, and it was great to hear his stories and get a taste of international rugby.

Clive had told the press that this 17-year-old lad, who had just made his debut for Warrington, could play in the game but both of us pretty much knew I wouldn't make the match day squad. As it turned out I was a sand boy for the match, taking it on when Jonathan Davies was kicking goals, but I was just glad to be involved.

Union and league were very different in those days. Now we see league players like Andy Farrell, Jason Robinson and, of course, myself move from league to union. But in 1993, union was still amateur and the only movement was one way, from union to league. Looking back at that first Wales squad, there were many familiar names for diehard union fans, players they would have supported through their union careers, before they turned professional and went north. For a kid who grew up watching the likes of Jonathan Davies, Allan Bateman and Rob Ackerman, just to see my name in the papers as part of the same squad was nothing short of magical. It was an incredible feeling to see the name I. Harris amongst those legends. A short time before I would have been happy to just go and watch some of these guys play. Now I was in the same squad as them. That first Wales squad, back in 1993, was: Rob Ackerman (Cardiff Institute ARL), Allan Bateman (Warrington), Gerald Cordle (Bradford Northern), Jonathan Davies (Warrington, capt.), John Devereux (Widnes), Kevin Ellis (Warrington), Phil Ford (Salford), Jonathan Griffiths (St Helens), Adrian Hadley (Widnes), Iestyn Harris (Warrington), Mark Jones (Hull), Paul Kennett (Swinton), Ian Marlow (Wakefield Trinity), Mark Moran (Leigh), Gary Pearce (Ryedale-York), Rowland Phillips (Warrington), Paul Reynolds (Widnes), Ian Stevens (Hull), Anthony Sullivan (St Helens), Barry Williams (Carlisle), Peter Williams (Salford), David Young (Salford). My ambition, up until then, had been to get in the Great Britain Academy side for Wembley but everything had happened so quickly that to be in the Welsh squad was more than I dared dream about.

Because of the small number of Welsh people playing league and the fact that so many of them had come from union, that Welsh team was almost like a club side.

The team line-up rarely changed, unless a new player arrived from union, and the atmosphere with them was unbelievable. If every national team could bottle what those guys had together they would be world-beaters.

I was lucky that there were a few Warrington players in the squad. They were the older heads, some of the catalysts of the team, so for me to have them on my side was a big thing. I felt they respected me right from the start. You can imagine what a thrill it was for a 17 year old like me to mix with and be accepted by those guys.

Like most young players, I was quiet when I first came into the squad. I think if you aren't quiet at the start you can come over as arrogant. I came in nice and quiet and people appreciated it. I looked up to those players and appreciated what they had done in the game. I would do anything for that team. I'd do the water bottles, carry the sand, anything that needed to be done.

I was in the dressing-room in the final few minutes before they ran out to face New Zealand in that international and I remember looking over at Anthony Sullivan, with whom I later played in union, for Cardiff, and seeing what great shape he was in physically. I remember thinking, 'Good God, I have a long way to go before I can match up to a player like him.' It would mean a lot of hard work and conditioning but it was good to be in the changing-rooms seeing what it was all about.

I was given a Wales kit which I've still got. It was all Puma and I remember the big box with the tracksuit and training gear with the three feathers on. To have that kit meant an awful lot to me; I was a very excited young man when I got that box in my hands.

The team went into camp for around four or five days and that was a really good experience for me. As a group of players they were so close and that contributed to an incredible atmosphere. It was almost like a set of friends meeting up to play rugby league because a lot of them had known each other from union days.

However, the friendliness didn't mean I couldn't be the subject of some good-natured fun. On that first trip with Wales my mum and dad wished me luck and sent me off with £100 pocket money for the weekend. Of course I made the mistake of mentioning this and on the coach down to Wales I was introduced to the skills of card playing by one Mr Paul Moriarty. What a character!

They really looked after 'the boy'. The only problem was that by the time we reached the team hotel I was on the phone to mum asking for more money. In teaching me the game, Mr Moriarty had taken over £80 off me. Great times!

I've never experienced what that group of players had. Even in my later years with Wales it was never as good as that. I suppose they were almost like ex-pats in a different country. The feeling in the squad was unique. We had a real laugh and the boys would always go out together, sometimes before games but always afterwards whether we won or lost.

I went out with them that week and it opened my eyes a little as to what team spirit really could be. Everyone was incredibly friendly and accepted me even though I was the youngster of the team, being a good five or six years younger than any of them.

Rugby league wasn't, and probably still isn't, prevalent in Wales so there weren't the youth players coming through. However, the influx of players from union meant it was a golden era for the Wales team, which continued until the 1995 World Cup.

In that year the union game turned professional and not only did the movements from union to league dry up but there were the beginnings of moves the other way.

While it was great being with the Welsh squad in 1993, I had to wait until 1994 to make my Wales debut, when Australia came over to the UK to play in a Test series against Great Britain. It was a full tour which included club matches and one Test against Wales.

I first pulled on that famous red jersey against the Wallabies on 30 October at Ninian Park, Cardiff. The experience was made all the easier by the time I had spent with the squad in the preceding year. This time I wasn't Jonathan's sand boy but rather his replacement as he had to pull out of the game with a shoulder injury. I think I would have played even if Jonathan hadn't got injured, but his absence meant I came in at stand-off.

Making my debut as an 18 year old was an honour but to then be selected at stand-off, rather than on the wing, ensured it would be extra special for me. Unlike at Warrington, where I simply took over his role as goalkicker, now I was taking his place at stand-off. I had started a couple of games there for Warrington but to be facing up to Australia in that position was fabulous. I was one of only four who weren't former union players, the others being Mark Perrett, Anthony Sullivan and Ian Marlow. Naturally, it was a big day out for the Harris family mum and dad, joining sister Rhiain and loads of my friends in the crowd.

From not even having a team to talk about a few years earlier, this Wales side had some massive names in it – John Devereux, Phil Ford, Gerald Cordle, Kevin Ellis and Paul Moriarty. It was a great team to come into, especially as a stand-off. I suppose in Wales rugby league was thought of as a second-tier sport but that didn't diminish the day for me. I was so proud to be standing there in my Wales jersey. Any game for Wales meant so much to me and that feeling grew because of the spirit in the team. We all knew it wouldn't last for ever, which meant that everyone was making the most of every opportunity that came our way.

Initially, I felt there was still some animosity in the Welsh public towards the team because so many of their rugby union heroes had been lost to league. All that had changed by the following season when we got magnificent, passionate support at the World Cup.

In the run-up to the game against Australia we not only lost Jonathan but Allan Bateman as well. Everyone expected both these guys to line up for Great Britain against the Australians again the following week, so we knew that without them we would be up against it. Before we had even got to the first quarter of the match we suffered another huge blow when John Devereux was carried off following a tackle from Mal Meninga, who at the time was the best centre in the world.

Devs went in and his jaw dropped onto Mal's shoulder. I know some sections of the media made a lot of that Meninga tackle, saying it was dirty play, but within the squad we didn't think that, it was just a massive hit. I was in and around the tackle on John and heard the crunch. I knew it was bad and I remember thinking how glad I was that it wasn't me. John himself knew it wasn't malicious and he was eventually diagnosed with a compound fracture of the jaw.

It was a very physical match and there was quite a lot of blood spilt. They were the world champions and before the game we had talked about how physical we would need to be to even things up a little. We said from the outset we would fire into them to see what they'd got. There were a few scraps breaking out all over the field. Kevin Ellis got caught early on and then John went off with his jaw injury. Dai Young left the field with his ear hanging off but then came back on! He also needed 12 stitches in a cut to his eye.

They had put out a terrific team and we went 30–0 down. It was only the massive team spirit in our side that ensured we didn't collapse completely in the second half. We ended up on the wrong side of a 46–4 defeat, Daio Powell diving on a loose ball to give us our try, one I don't think anyone could have begrudged us. That was by far the most physical game of my career so far and it was good to know I could stand up to a game at that level. Although we lost, I look back on it with fondness. Dai Young was captain at the time and he made a big effort with me. There were quite a few young lads in the team alongside me, and Dai was a calming influence for all of us. Everyone had great respect for him. He was not one of those union players who you'd have said would make it in league but you have to give him all the credit in the world for making that bold move, particularly as not many props went north. But he did extremely well in his league career. He was one of those players who had a tough reputation and could stand up for himself. He had a little bit of stick when he first came but he got through it. There were loads of stories about people trying to take him on and coming off second best! Once they realised that they left him alone to get on with his career.

It was clearly a tough day for me, but as the *Independent* report put it, I think I acquitted myself pretty well. It said:

> Iestyn Harris, given the awesome task of replacing Davies as stand-off and goal-kicker, missed the conversion, but did better than could be reasonably expected with his responsibility of standing in for the irreplaceable . . . Harris is only 18 and normally plays on the wing but he was a committed, courageous and skilful stand-off.

The writing was on the wall from the time that the

Welsh coach, Clive Griffiths, confirmed what everyone had
long suspected – that Jonathan Davies and Allan Bateman
would not play.

I had to wait until the following February – 1995 – for my first
win in a Wales shirt and what a win, against England, again at
Ninian Park, in the European Championship. It was our first
victory over them in 18 years.

This is one of the games that will stick with me for a long time.
It was a very good England team. They were confident, bordering
on arrogant, going into that game. Wales weren't really a
dominant force and we certainly thought they believed they
would steamroller us.

From the opening minutes you could see it was going to be a
torrid, physical battle and it was. They had some tough players, as
did we, so it was just tit for tat for most of the game. I remember
a couple of 26-man brawls, so it must have been a nightmare to
referee as it got very tasty. Kevin Ellis took a bit of a beating and
ended up with a few stitches and a couple of black eyes. Dai
Young obviously sorted a few out, as did Paul Moriarty. They
didn't take any rubbish.

I played in the centre in that game as Jonathan was at stand-off.
It turned into one of the most memorable games of my career
and crucial at the time with the World Cup on the horizon. We
were 16–8 down with 17 minutes to play. Kevin Ellis then scored
a try and Jonathan kicked the conversion before landing two drop
goals to bring us home. That match signalled that Wales had
arrived in rugby league; it put us on the map as an international
team and ensured we'd be a dangerous side at the following
World Cup.

One thing you could guarantee was that this Wales team was
going to have a big celebration after the game. This side knew
everyone in Cardiff and we toured the bars like kings. We also had
the luxury of not being under too much press scrutiny as we were
a rugby league side in union territory. We had a good time

without having any problems and I know some of the rugby union guys coming to league saw this as a real privilege because they were used to being continually under the spotlight in union.

The teams for that historic England v. Wales clash were: *Wales*: Paul Atcheson (Wigan); Phil Ford (Salford), Allan Bateman (Warrington), Iestyn Harris (Warrington), Anthony Sullivan (St Helens); Jonathan Davies (Warrington; capt.), Kevin Ellis (Workington Town); Kelvin Skerrett (Wigan), Martin Hall (Wigan), David Young (Salford), Paul Moriarty (Halifax), Mark Perrett (Halifax), Richie Eyres (Leeds). Subs: Neil Cowie (Wigan), Rowland Phillips (Workington Town), Adrian Hadley (Widnes), Daio Powell (Wakefield Trinity). *England*: Richard Gay (Hull); Jason Robinson (Wigan), Daryl Powell (Sheffield Eagles), Paul Newlove (Bradford Northern), Ikram Butt (Featherstone Rovers); Garry Schofield (Leeds), Deryck Fox (Bradford Northern); Karl Harrison (Halifax), Richard Russell (Castleford), Harvey Howard (Leeds), Anthony Farrell (Sheffield Eagles), Sonny Nickle (St Helens), Phil Clarke (Wigan; capt.). Subs: Steve McCurrie (Widnes), Mick Cassidy (Wigan), Simon Baldwin (Halifax), Steve McNamara (Hull).

Later that month, we completed a great season when we clinched the European Championship, for the first time since 1938, with a 22–10 win over France in Carcassonne. It was an extra special night for me as the game marked my first try for Wales, which cancelled out an earlier one from them. I was on the wing and I remember it being the coldest and wettest day of my life. There were huge puddles all over the pitch and people were sliding left, right and centre. I slid about 30 metres to score my try! I went over in the corner and just kept on going well over the dead ball line.

It was so cold we all headed for the changing-rooms as soon as the final whistle blew. In the presentation pictures you can see the cold in Jonathan's eyes. It wasn't helped by the fact that he was probably the only one left out there – everyone else was in the showers warming up.

The games with Wales, while they obviously meant a lot to me, were pretty low-key affairs, although that was all to change in 1995 when we played in the World Cup. The tournament was magnificent, played against a backdrop of the break-up of that Wales team. Everyone knew that because union had just turned professional it would only be a matter of time before some of the Welsh players were tempted back to the 15-a-side game. Cardiff had already talked with Jonathan and Phil Ford of Salford.

I was also on their wanted list and this was when the first thoughts of a career in union and league started to materialise in my mind.

I could have gone with that first wave of players and was flattered by the early attention those performances at the World Cup had brought me and the interest it generated from rugby union clubs. Shortly after the tournament there were a few inquiries, one from Cardiff and another from Llanelli. They were offering me good money, certainly more than I was on at Warrington, so it was very tempting. I was also approached by Terry Cobner, on behalf of the WRU, to do the sort of deal I eventually did in 2001. Terry came up to see me to find out if I was interested in moving down to south Wales. They were offering me almost double the salary I was on at Warrington. I did consider it but I was pretty honest with him and said I didn't feel the time was right. I was 19 and knew I had so much more to achieve in league.

After the World Cup, I signed a new contract with Warrington which was worth £15,000 a year. That would make me a full-time player on the third highest contract at the club, and that's why I gave up my A levels. League salaries ranged from £10,000 to £20,000 but obviously the stars were on quite a bit more.

I suppose the interest from Wales was understandable given that I was the first Welsh player to have grown up playing league. Even at that young age I knew I wanted to play union in Wales one day. Clearly, being born in Oldham would qualify me to play for England but to be honest that never entered my head. It would be like asking Jason Robinson if he'd like to play for Wales rather than England. He'd think you were mad to ask and it was the same for me.

Rugby league was about to become a summer game with the advent of Super League and some people suggested that players could play all the year round, league in the summer and union in winter. Part of me would have loved to have given it a go and I thought it was a real possibility. As a 19 year old, I thought I could do it all. The idea of playing rugby 12 months a year appealed to me, particularly if I could play in the then Five Nations Championship. People talked about burn-out, but show me a 19-year-old sportsman who has burn-out on his mind.

After the European Championship victory, it was time to turn our attention to the World Cup. It was a great tournament. All my friends came and watched every game and we had some great nights out!

Mike Nicholas, the Wales team manager, was friends with the owner of one particular bar, Winston's, so we often ended up there at the end of a big night out.

I know some people had a stuffy attitude to these nights out and there was some criticism for us having one or two beers, but at that time that was just how it was.

The game has moved on but you have to remember that this team was unique. There was a bit of the Harlem Globetrotters about the side, lots of big names playing with the right attitude. The drinking culture had been there in rugby union and many of the lads had moved over to league without leaving that behind. The enjoyment factor, though, was huge and we really saw how the Welsh public could get behind a team.

Before the World Cup we enjoyed a quick trip to America where we played and won two Tests, spending ten days in Philadelphia. I made some good mates on that tour, including Keiron Cunningham, the St Helens hooker. He was 17 at the time and already an outstanding player who became my long-time room-mate.

As a squad, we were together for five weeks prior to the World Cup and it was probably the best five weeks of my professional career. We stayed in the same hotel, in the centre of Cardiff, The Post House, and we built up a great team spirit. We worked very hard on the training field and in the matches.

Our first match was against France at Ninian Park and drew 10,250 fans, the biggest crowd for a Welsh game since 1991. There were three-mile queues outside the ground and the start had to be delayed by 15 minutes. 'Come and see a real dragon fly,' the posters proclaimed, and they did. The number of fans was far more than we expected and the team were delighted at the way the public were taking to us. Their passion had gone up a notch and we knew we had to get off to a good start.

If we'd made a poor start the support may have drifted away but luckily for us everything went well against France. The French had come on a lot since we beat them in the European Championship and it was quite tight for a long time. To their credit, they seemed as inspired as us and came out firing, trying to impose their physical game on us. Anthony Sullivan scored two tries in the first half with me having a hand in both. Jonathan added two goals to give us a 12–0 half-time lead.

I'll never forget my try in the second half, as I got home from 45 yards and we won 28–6, our fourth victory over the French in three years. Suddenly people sat up and took notice and the odds against us winning the competition were slashed from 25–1 to 14–1.

In the run-up to that World Cup, league had seen the emergence of former union players like Scott Gibbs and Scott Quinnell into genuine talents, and with players like Jonathan Davies, John Devereux, Allan Bateman, Anthony Sullivan and Kevin Ellis, I suppose it wasn't surprising we caught the imagination of the Welsh public. The team that day was: Iestyn Harris (Warrington); John Devereux (Widnes), Allan Bateman (Cronulla), Scott Gibbs (St Helens), Anthony Sullivan (St Helens); Jonathan Davies (Warrington; capt.), Kevin Ellis (North Queensland Cowboys); Kelvin Skerrett (Wigan), Martin Hall

(Wigan), David Young (Salford), Paul Moriarty (Halifax), Mark Perrett (Halifax), Richie Eyres (Leeds). Subs: Adrian Hadley (Widnes), Mark Jones (Warrington), Keiron Cunningham (St Helens), Rowland Phillips (Workington Town).

I was a humble member of that side, yet no matter how old you were or what background you came from, everyone was treated the same. Clive Griffiths played a big part as coach. He treated men like men and didn't try to order anyone around. Throughout my career wherever I have gone, so has Clive. It's been great to have him around.

Wales manager Mike Nicholas was also a big supporter of mine at the time and he, very flatteringly, compared me to a player who had made a huge impression almost a quarter of a century before, Barry John. Mike said, 'I can see shades of Barry in Iestyn every time I watch him play. The try he scored for us against France was one Barry would have been proud of. This kid has to get better. He was 19 only in June and has already been man of the match against Australia and now France. He is contracted to Warrington for another four years but he fancies playing union at some stage and will still only be 23. Iestyn would walk into the Wales team if he ever decided to move across.'

I didn't get carried away with what he said, as I knew I wasn't in the same league as Barry John.

We moved from the victory over France to selling out another football ground, this time packing more than 15,000 into Swansea City's Vetch Field when we took on Western Samoa. I gather a few hundred people were locked out of the match. Who would have believed, a few years earlier, that a rugby league match could sell out a football ground in south Wales?

The temperature at Swansea on that Sunday was red hot. I had never experienced a more passionate occasion. The singing was incredible and the passion from the crowd must have been worth at least ten points to us. I remember someone told me there were some seats in the stand at Swansea that hadn't been sat on in all of ten years.

Martin Hall said he was so moved he had goose pimples.

It was an emotional night in many ways as we realised that not only would it be our last game in Wales for a while – the semi-final was at Old Trafford – but for a few players it would be their last in Wales. For Jonathan, it was likely to be his last game of international rugby league in Wales.

Those factors were a big motivation going into the game and were significant in giving us the resilience to overcome an impressive Samoan team. In 1991 the Samoans had famously upset the odds and beaten the Wales rugby union side in the World Cup. We had no intention of going the same way.

We had gone to watch Samoa take on France the Wednesday before, at Ninian Park. We knew they would be physical and they put 56 points on France, confirming what tough opponents they were going to be. Seeing them gave us a wake-up call.

I remember going into the changing-rooms at the Vetch, which I don't think were designed for a squad of rugby league players, and being told that the kick-off had been delayed 15 minutes due to crowd congestion. Then it started to dawn on us what a big game this was for the Welsh public. The crowd are completely on top of you at the Vetch and extremely loud so it created a magical atmosphere.

Samoa had a huge team with league legends like Va'aiga Tuigamala but the Welsh pack to a man were outstanding – they had to be. From the kick-off, there were big hits going in left, right and centre. Scott Quinnell was massive for us. He hadn't played for a few months but he gave everything that day, putting his body on the line. He was the obvious choice as man of the match and it was probably the first time people started to talk about Scott Quinnell, the rugby league player, rather than Scott Quinnell, the rugby union player.

It was the most physical match I had ever been involved in, even more so than England in the European Championship. You know what Samoans are like. They are big, big men, very physical and they expected to bowl us out of the way. But I don't think they realised how big a side we had and Jonathan came up with a couple of special plays.

I was at full-back and lucky enough to get on the score sheet with a try from the first scrum, dummying across the line. It was excellent to get the first score. The crowd went crazy when Kevin Ellis found a gap on the left and scored in the corner, and I even dropped a goal in the last minute. We won 22–10 and many people thought it was Wales's best performance since the side was resurrected in 1991. We finished top of Group Three with four points which set us up for a huge showdown with England, at Old Trafford.

After the games in Wales had finished, my family and friends from Oldham, including Darren Morgan, my best friend, came to the team hotel in Cardiff. We had all been out and returned to a party in the residents' bar. It was packed and we had a great night. I remember everyone being overwhelmed by the generosity of Paul Moriarty. He was buying drinks for everyone but after a few hours of Paul insisting he got all the drinks, my dad finally had had enough and said, 'No, Paul, you can't keep buying everyone drinks!' To which Paul replied, 'It's no problem, Mr Harris, I'm putting it all on Iestyn's room!' And he was! Priceless!

We probably celebrated a little bit too hard, the celebrations going on through Sunday and Monday. All the senior players decided they wanted to stay in Wales until later in the week. The theory was that we could have a better time in Cardiff. Looking back, it was a mistake: we didn't prepare as well for the semi-final as we did for the other two games and perhaps it cost us.

England were, of course, far better than they had been in the European Championship. Gary Connolly missed that tournament, severely hampering the chances of Phil Larder's side, and he'd even lost his captain, Shaun Edwards, halfway through, so we knew it would be a completely different England this time around.

We were 12–0 down before we had broken sweat and we were always chasing the game. We got back to within six points but although I thought we gave a good account of ourselves, it was perhaps one game too far for us. On the day, their defence was also immense. We'd had a brutal game a few days earlier, against Samoa, and they'd had an easy game.

It was a feisty encounter. The bigger pitch meant it was a more open game whereas we would have liked it tighter. I remember Anthony Sullivan, who was on fire at the time, leaving Jason Robinson for dead down the touchline. We certainly had the players who could, and should, have beaten England but in the end we just fell short. Martin Offiah scored two very controversial tries. He dropped one from about a foot off the floor and it was given, then he scored again, dropping another one over the line. Television replays proved we were right to question the validity of those scores but it was just before the advent of the video referee so there was nothing we could do. We ended up losing 25–10.

I expected them to target me as I was new to the full-back role. Clive pulled me aside and said I needed to be aware I might get more attention than normal but I was fine with that. True to form, the high bombs arrived once we kicked off.

We never really got into the game, which was a huge disappointment. Everyone accepted we had done well to get that far but deep down we were disappointed as we felt we could have done better. In the following week, as the build-up to the World Cup final started in earnest, more and more of us felt that it should have been us. It still hurts me today. We showed in that European Championship game that we could beat England, so to see them go on to play Australia in the final was galling. It should have been us and we knew it!

That game really felt like the end of an era and there were a few tears flowing as we all knew this team would never take the field again. For players like Jonathan it was to be their last international. Over 10,000 Welsh fans had made the trip to Manchester and as we did a lap of honour at the end it was a magnificent sight. It was the first time a sizeable number of fans had travelled from Wales to watch the rugby league side. I only wish we could have delivered a victory for them to celebrate.

It was an honour to pull on the Wales jersey in that World Cup and even after it had finished I was further honoured as one of only two Wales players, along with Anthony Sullivan, to be selected in the team of the tournament, which was: Iestyn Harris (Wal); Jason Robinson (Eng), Paul Newlove (Eng), Richie Blackmore (NZ), Anthony Sullivan (Wal); Brad Fittler (Aus), Adrian Lam (PNG); Mark Carroll (Aus), Lee Jackson (Eng), David Westley (PNG), Denis Betts (Eng), Steve Menzies (Aus), Andy Farrell (Eng). I was also named International Player of the Year at the same time.

Being just 19, I was shocked to see how fast things were moving. After the World Cup I was aware that I had moved up a stage in my career. The World Cup was a watershed for me. Once I returned to Warrington I was going into games with far more confidence, believing in my abilities because of the way I grew up in that tournament. I thought I had matured a lot in five weeks.

The physicality of the games was important but I think a lot of the work I had done between the ages of 16 and 19 on the training field and in the gym was starting to pay off. Physically I was starting to catch up. Once I got back from the World Cup, I was looking across at players from my own team and the opposition and thinking that they were not necessarily way ahead of me.

There was a huge state of flux in rugby league, with an unprecedented number of moves. The 1995 World Cup was the perfect opportunity for rugby league to have kicked on and set itself up as a viable sport in south Wales. The crowds we got in that competition and the obvious interest that the Welsh public took in our games proved that rugby league had a future in the Principality. I know many of those supporters were there because the Wales side was full of former union heroes but within the squad we detected that the interest went deeper than that and that league could have taken off.

I still believe, had the backing come through, we could have seen the establishment of a side in Wales. Many of the former union players in league would have loved to have 'gone home' and where better than to a league side in south Wales? For me it was a personal disappointment that a south Wales team could not get off the ground as I would genuinely like to have played for them in Super League. It would have been the perfect combination for me, learning my craft in Super League while representing Wales every week, in a side that would have become as near as you could get to the national side. In the right place, you'd have had a lot of Welsh players who'd want to play for that team.

Many of those Welsh players had returned to union over the following years so by the time of the next Rugby League World Cup in 2000 it was a side full of dyed-in-the-wool rugby league players. The 1995 World Cup was special. The 2000 World Cup was good but the only ones left from 1995 were myself, Keiron Cunningham and Anthony Sullivan. We reached the semi-final again but it just wasn't the same as 1995. That special group of players could never be assembled again.

In 2000, although we enjoyed it, the Welsh public didn't take to us in the same way as they had done five years before. We didn't have the ex-union players like Jonathan Davies, Scott Gibbs and Scott Quinnell. We didn't capture the imagination of the public, which was disappointing.

As I mentioned, there were only three survivors from the team that had lost in the semi-final to England five years before so you can appreciate how daunting a task we faced. But I believed from day one we had the quality in the team to get to the semi-finals again. If we gelled, and it was a big if in those days, I knew we could be every bit as competitive, especially after a good training week in South Africa.

We went into the tournament with only one Welsh-born player, St Helens' reserve forward Gareth Price, but players like Anthony Farrell and Paul Sterling gave us real rugby league quality. Anthony was a really tough forward, which is just what we needed, and with Paul Sterling on one wing and Anthony Sullivan on the other we had real pace. The full squad – in 2000 – was: Paul Atcheson (St Helens), Lee Briers (Warrington), Dean Busby (Warrington), Garreth Carvell (Hull), Neil Cowie (Wigan), Jason Critchley (Leicester RU), Keiron Cunningham (St Helens), Wes Davies (Wigan), Barry Eaton (Dewsbury), Anthony Farrell (Leeds), Damian Gibson (Halifax), Karle Hammond (Widnes), Iestyn Harris (Leeds, capt.), Paul Highton (Salford), Mick Jenkins (Hull), Justin Morgan (Canberra), Chris Morley (Sheffield), Gareth Price (St Helens), Chris Smith (St Helens), Paul Sterling (Leeds), Anthony Sullivan (St Helens), Kris Tassell (Salford), Ian Watson (Widnes), Dave Whittle (Leigh).

We had quality in our side and I remember being angry at the fact that were quoted as 80–1 outsiders to win it. Obviously we would have to overcome world champions Australia to do it but 80–1? I didn't understand that! I was disappointed at some of the comments that were made. People were saying Wales were a weak side, but we had strength in depth.

We played at Llanelli on a freezing cold night and there were about 900 people there to watch us beat Lebanon 24–22. Teams like Lebanon and Russia made it into the World Cup as, building on the success of 1995, it was decided to expand the format further, with the number of teams rising from 10 to 16. Unfortunately that meant too many mismatches in the group stages. Australia beat Russia 110–4 and New Zealand beat Lebanon 64–0.

We were in Group Two, with New Zealand, and we kicked off with a 38–6 win over the Cook Islands before losing to the Kiwis 58–18. We finished second in our group and went into the quarter-finals where the Papua New Guineans were waiting for us.

PNG had an excellent team at the time. We played them at Widnes and they were expected to beat us, but we won that game as well, both Kieron Cunningham and Anthony Sullivan having great games to take us home. The key for us was that the experienced players in the squad were playing well. In addition to

Kieron and Anthony, Lee Briers from Warrington stepped up.

We drew Australia in the semi-final and we went into the game as 7–1 outsiders. Clive moved me to full-back and most people predicted we would lose by 60 points. Little did they know this Wales team was made of sterner stuff. We certainly gave the Aussies a shock and at half-time were six points ahead. This was the same Australian team that had put 66 points past the Samoans in the quarter-final and scored 198 points in their three group games!

I remember that dressing-room at half-time as if it were yesterday. We had a load of young players in our squad and I could tell by the looks on their faces that they were getting carried away. They were thinking: 'This is it, we are going to beat Australia.' Oh, if only it were that simple! Myself, Kieron and Anthony were fully aware that, with us six points up, we hadn't seen anything like the best of the Kangaroos yet. We knew the onslaught that was waiting for us in the second half, as we'd had experience of taking on these players many times before. We tried to calm everyone down and explain that we needed to settle down and go onto that field for the second half as if we were starting again. We had been involved in too many matches when a six-point lead had disappeared in a flash.

You can, of course, catch a side like Australia on the hop in one half, but to do it again was going to take world-class performances from every player in a Wales shirt. We handed Australia another fright by scoring again to make it 22–14 and I think the younger players in the squad got a little too excited. Incredibly, Australia didn't take the lead until the 58th minute, so you can see how close we were to what would have been one of the biggest shocks in the history of rugby league. After all, we came into the tournament as massive outsiders!

But it wasn't to be. We gave a few penalties away and they got on a roll. In the end, although we battled bravely and couldn't have asked any more of any member of our team, we came up short. They beat us 46–22.

The Australians admitted afterwards that they had 'disrespected' us. Prop Shane Webcke said, 'In the back of our heads we were all thinking more about next week than we were this week, and we probably disrespected them a bit and we got our bums kicked a bit for it.'

Clive Griffiths was proud of the performance and pleased with my switch of position for the game. If anyone knew I could move to full-back, it was Clive. He said, 'Tactically, we did things that surprised the Australians and we went out to do that intentionally. A few eyebrows were raised when we put Harris at full-back, but things worked, and for 60 minutes we dreamt, didn't we? We had a number of decisions against us which I've got a question mark on one or two of them. They got a roll on and we didn't touch the ball.'

Those boys on duty that day, in the red shirt of Wales, should, however, take an enormous amount of pride and credit from that performance. Everyone had expected to see us slaughtered and we ended up taking the best team in the world right to the wire. There were about 10,000 at the stadium in Huddersfield and we received a standing ovation at the end as those fans realised what we had done. No one had come that close in the tournament, not even New Zealand in the final, and the Australian players were happy to acknowledge that afterwards. They were coming up to us, shaking our hands and saying, 'You gave us the fright of our lives.'

We may have lost to New Zealand and Australia in 2000 but I don't want to underestimate what we did achieve and what an honour it was for me to captain my country in a World Cup. Anthony Sullivan was a massive help as my vice-captain and the boys pulled together really well for us to make the last four – no mean achievement.

That semi-final defeat to Australia ended up being my last game for the Wales rugby league team. I missed the match against England at the Racecourse Ground in July 2001. Games in between World Cups for Wales were few and far between.

I had desperately wanted to play against England but in the summer of 2001 I had to have exploratory surgery on the wrist I injured after crashing into an advertising hoarding at Bradford. As I was captain, however, it was important for me to be with the squad. I could have had the operation on the day before the match, but I'd opted to have it on the day after so that I could stay with them. In the end I acted as a water carrier for the team. I started my Wales rugby league career as Jonathan Davies' sand boy and ended it, at least temporarily when I moved to union, as a water carrier.

The side battled bravely on that night in Wrexham, eventually going down 42–33 to an England side captained by Andy Farrell. In many ways the performance had been staggering, considering how many problems the coach Neil Kelly had encountered in putting the team together.

In addition to my memorable career with Wales, I was also lucky enough to play for Great Britain. My Great Britain career started during my time at Warrington when Phil Larder took a squad to Papua New Guinea and New Zealand in 1997.

At the time I was in dispute with Warrington and training at all hours, so the call from Great Britain was not only an honour, it also allowed me to get away from the club!

That was a tough debut, though. It was around 100 degrees and a couple of the lads suffered heat exhaustion. The ground officially held about 6,000 people, although there were probably about 26,000 there on the day. Rugby league is the national sport in PNG and there were people up in trees and climbing up the fences. A few even fell out of the trees at one point. They were used to the heat and we definitely weren't, but we scraped through to a win. I had long dreamed of making my Great Britain debut but never thought it would happen in Papua New Guinea under those conditions.

Phil Larder was great with me. I have always got on with him professionally and personally. He has never been anything but honest with me and it was good to see him again when I moved to union and played against England in the Six Nations and the World Cup.

It was a huge thrill for me to play for GB on that trip. It was a great tour and there were a lot of good players. The team for my GB debut was: Stuart Spruce (Bradford); Joey Hayes (St Helens), Kris Radlinski (Wigan), Alan Hunte (St Helens), Anthony Sullivan (St Helens); Iestyn Harris (Warrington), Bobbie Goulding (St Helens); Paul Broadbent (Sheffield Eagles), Keiron Cunningham (St Helens), Terry O'Connor (Wigan), Denis Betts (Wigan), Chris Joynt (St Helens), Andy Farrell (Wigan; capt.). Subs: Tony Smith (Castleford), Rowland Phillips (Workington Town), Daryl Powell (Keighley Cougars), Paul Sculthorpe (Warrington). We lost all three Tests in New Zealand, coming up short by a couple of points in each. We could have won all three, but we did beat Papua New Guinea and Fiji and I played stand-off in all the games.

During the turmoil at Warrington, I was also picked to play in the World Nines in Townsville, Australia. We did really well and got to the semi-finals. At this stage, I was almost clubless, coming back from this trip to a 4 a.m. training routine.

My last game for Great Britain, before my move to union, had come two years before when I was selected for the Tri-Nations series, in Auckland, 1999. We finished the trip with a 24–6 defeat to New Zealand, in Auckland, a record losing margin against New Zealand in 97 Tests. I didn't even have the satisfaction of finishing that last game – a torn groin muscle put paid to that ambition. But luckily that wasn't my last taste of Test match rugby league as I was able to return to the international stage in 2004 for the Gillette Tri-Nations series in the UK.

FOUR

ONE DOOR CLOSES, ANOTHER ONE OPENS

From as early as I can remember, I dreamed of being a professional rugby player. I was always imagining how it would feel to run out at places like Central Park, Odsal, Headingley and Cardiff Arms Park. But I certainly didn't imagine that any career I had in rugby would involve me getting up at 3.30 a.m. to start training at 4 on my own. But that is what faced me in my final days at Warrington, the club I had joined as a 15 year old, the club where I enjoyed so many happy days.

In 1994, I had signed a contract with Warrington, worth £15,000, which made me the third highest player on their books. That gives you an idea of what most rugby league players were on at that time but that pay structure was to change overnight with the arrival of Rupert Murdoch's millions in 1995.

In a move to enable his television company in Australia to show rugby league, Murdoch had introduced a new competition called Super League, made up of some already established clubs alongside several new franchises. He proposed a Super League in Britain of 12 clubs who would all be fully professional but the game had to switch to summer. In

April 1995, the Rugby Football League accepted £87 million to do just that.

However, in Australia, the ARL, who ran the game there, fought back and began signing players for their own long-established competition, which included recruiting some of Britain's star players. This developed into a bidding war between the ARL and Super League, with the winners being the British players.

I was happy with my £15,000 club contract one minute and then the next I was getting offered close to £100,000, all in the space of a day. Many players became rich overnight. Good luck to those who signed, but, as I will explain, the deal just wasn't right for me at the time, no matter what they were offering.

I was probably two years too young to get the big money but the likes of Jason Robinson, Jonathan Davies and Andy Farrell were getting offered ridiculous sums of money and all power to them. It was amazing and to be honest it came from nowhere.

Jonathan signed for the ARL in Australia before changing his mind and moving back to Cardiff, as one of the first high-profile union signings after the game went professional in 1995.

I was one of a number of players to be offered a ludicrous contract with the ARL. The deal was for £100,000 a year (nearly seven times my salary at Warrington) but I would have to give up the right to play international rugby since the British game was wholly allied to Murdoch's Super League. The people advising me said it was the right deal and for me to take it and I suppose, looking at it from the outside, it was. The offer was around £75,000 up front, which was paid there and then as soon as I signed – that was in addition to the £100,000 a year, for four years. A little different to what I was currently on at Warrington!

But I refused to sign – further proof that I wasn't, and never have been, motivated by money.

They were trying to get all the best players in the world in their competition and I gather they offered other more established players as much as £750,000 in a lump sum to go to the ARL. If you signed, they wrote the cheque in front of you and handed it over before the ink was dry on the contract. It was that bizarre.

A lot of players signed with them and then a big legal wrangle went on and everything was pushed to one side. But the players were able to keep those signing-on fees, so a group of them received a massive lump sum for doing absolutely nothing. They simply took the money and didn't have to do anything for it. There were players who became very wealthy men for literally staying exactly where they were.

Had I signed, I would have fulfilled my contract with Warrington, which had about two years left, and then gone to Australia where I would have been placed with an Australian club, although at the time I wasn't told which one.

On one occasion I went to a solicitor's office in Bradford to have a look at my contract and players were emerging from there punching the air with big cheques in their hands. They were saying, 'You won't believe what I've been offered,' and walking out with huge smiles on their faces. They'd go in expecting maybe a £30,000 to £40,000 bonus and then be offered £300,000 to £400,000. The offices felt like a dentist's waiting-room, with four or five players sitting outside waiting to go in and hear what they were being offered.

At 19, I was still relatively young when I walked into that office. I had missed the really big money, the half a million or quarter of a million signing-on fees, but I still got offered a good deal and I remember asking for 24 hours to think about it.

In that 24 hours, I rang Clive Griffiths, who was Warrington and Wales coach at the time. He was also a good friend, so I wanted to know what he thought. I told Clive that their contract stipulated that I had to end my international career and at 19, with a World Cup just behind me, it wasn't something I wanted to do. I also concluded that to accept the lump sum offered would mean that I was in breach of my contract with Warrington. I had no reason to leave Warrington as I was happy there.

Clive Griffiths' response was immediate. He took me down to the rugby league offices to meet the Super League people and they offered me a £50,000 signing-on fee with a substantial jump in my contract, to £70,000 a year. That was still some way off the deal the ARL were offering but a substantial increase in my current contract. I was one of the first to sign for Super League and it meant I could stay exactly where I was, which is what I wanted. Staying in England gave me a smaller salary but so many other things.

The whole saga didn't end there for me as I was then asked to give evidence on behalf of Super League, who were trying to put together a case against the ARL. Super League asked me to sign an affidavit confirming that I was told I would need to sign away my rights to international rugby. This could be seen as a restraint of trade and their case was that no one should be able to stop you playing international rugby.

The battle between the ARL and Super League raged in the middle of 1995, and for a while I was caught right in the middle of it. Maurice Lindsay, the RFL's chief executive, said:

> We must face it, they are breaking the law of the land and the courts will not accept it. When players sign contracts, they agree to abide by the RFL by-laws, which state that they must make themselves available for international selection. If players are paid any money whatsoever not to play for their country, I regard it as absolutely disgraceful.
>
> We are disappointed that they are targeting young players in the same despicable way they tried to stop Iestyn Harris from playing for his country.
>
> Super League has played by the rules and will not stoop to the dirty tricks at their level. The ARL are thumbing their noses at the English League and English law court judges.

To be honest, most of the rugby league players were in a state of disbelief as their salaries changed overnight, and all this money was being bandied about. Even those who were 33 or 34 and coming to the end of their careers were getting offered ridiculous amounts of money at a time when they must have been thinking their best earning days were over. It was great for them but the money did send the game into a bit of flux. No one knew the market value of players and they didn't know how to start negotiations, so with two competing factions at work, I suppose the contracts were always going to go through the roof. I know of players who accepted deals which were 20 times what they normally would have been on.

There was also speculation at the time that Welsh rugby union clubs were again coming in to offer me a pathway into a new sport. I'd had a couple of approaches from Welsh clubs a few weeks before, but I hadn't heard from the WRU directly, and I certainly hadn't been offered the £70,000 package about which some people had been speculating. Six months prior to this, playing union wasn't a possibility because it was still amateur but after the World Cup and union's move to professionalism it was.

I was a big supporter of Super League. I know there were many sceptics, especially as it meant rugby league becoming a summer sport, but I thought from the start it was great for the game. It improved things dramatically overnight and changed everything we knew about rugby league in England. It changed the way the players thought about their sport as they knew they had to get fitter and better or they wouldn't survive. The change was radical but it was a great idea and did so much for the sport. All you miss now are the cold months, which is no bad thing.

Also, it put a stop to people playing their winter in England and then their off-seasons in Australia, which the Australians were doing in reverse. Players were coming over here for mini-seasons in the winter and not really putting anything tangible into the game. Super League ended that and ensured players were more committed to one club, and to the sport in general. I think it is the best thing that has happened to the sport.

I suppose the beginning of the end for me at Warrington came in January 1996, at the conclusion of the final season of winter rugby league and not long after those great days at the World Cup with Wales.

The 1995–96 season was to be a shortened one, beginning in August and finishing in the middle of January, The new Super League was due to kick off in March and a whole new era in rugby league was about to begin. On 4 January, we travelled to play St Helens in the Regal Trophy semi-final and ended up getting thumped 80–0. Their captain, Bobbie Goulding, was in great form and they went on to rattle up a record semi-final score in our worst-ever defeat. That led to one of the worst things that could have happened to me, the departure of both Brian Johnson and Clive Griffiths. Both men had been so supportive of me during my career but they were now heading out of the Wilderspool gates for the last time.

Brian was the longest-serving coach in the British game at that time and he was working to a long-term plan. Since the club's 1990 Wembley defeat by Wigan, he had been concentrating on a youth policy from which I was lucky enough to benefit.

It was one of those absolutely bizarre games, and to this day I don't know where that 80–0 performance came from. We were full of confidence and had a full side and even started the match well, strangely enough. We had a good couple of sets early on but then it all went wrong.

They scored, we kicked off, they scored, we kicked off and they scored. They were soon 18–0 ahead. The game had gone and a few heads went down. We just couldn't stop them and Goulding also kicked the goals from everywhere. We came into the changing-rooms after the game and Brian just didn't say a word, which was very unusual for him – it was that bad!

He wasn't a ranter and a raver, and would never come in with all guns blazing but when we lost he would have his say and normally explain exactly why we had lost. He was an emotional guy and we always knew the way he was thinking just by looking at his facial expressions. But this time there was nothing. Silence is often far more powerful than the hairdryer treatment. I think a scoreline like 80–0 for a professional side like Warrington is beyond anger.

At the post-match press conference, Brian said, 'I would never have believed that in my worst nightmares. They were brilliant, but we were absolutely woeful.'

And in *The Independent*, Dave Hadfield wrote, 'It was some consolation to Warrington that the game's postponement from Saturday saved them from television exposure.' The only saving grace he could find was that our 80–0 defeat wasn't on television. That just about summed it up!

The mood was dragged down even further, if that were possible, when the chairman of the club, Peter Higham, came in and said how disgusted he was with the performance. In the whole of my career I can't remember a chairman coming into a dressing-room like that and laying into the players.

We got on the bus and I remember Brian came and sat at the back next to a group of us. Normally someone, even after a defeat, breaks the ice but that day it was different. There was almost total silence. Most of us were just hanging our heads in shame. He started chatting about life in general and we couldn't make head nor tail of it. At the time, I didn't see the significance of what Brian was saying.

But at 9 a.m. the next day, when we were called into the changing-rooms for a meeting, we understood. We had thought we'd been called in to go through the video and start putting what was wrong in the game right. We were sitting there and Brian came in, shocking everyone by telling us he had resigned the night before and his resignation had been accepted. I felt so sorry for him.

I remember him telling a story about the advent of Super League. One Saturday he had set up training for the following Tuesday and Thursday, to prepare for a game the next weekend. Then he was told that everyone would be in at 9 a.m. on Monday and there would be 32 full-time professionals looking for him to lead them.

Brian went from running a squad of 20 players with training on Tuesday and Thursday nights, to having 32 full-timers 7 days a week.

When Brian told us of his resignation, it left us in the most bizarre atmosphere I have ever experienced. For the next 20 minutes, you had about 30 players sitting in silence. Nobody moved or said a word as the news of Brian's departure began to sink in.

You must remember that many of us saw Brian as a father figure and he had a lot of respect in that dressing-room. I, in particular, owed him so much and after the defeat at St Helens we all felt we'd let him down. That dressing-room that morning was a horrible place to be, and it was a very tough time for the club. I thought back to my early days at Warrington as a 16 year old and all the help Brian had given me. When he needed me, I couldn't help him.

Clive Griffiths took over in the interim but although he applied for the job it was decided by the club that he wasn't the man to take us into the new era. He had been an assistant for so long under Brian but the club clearly wanted a clean sweep. However, I thought Clive would have done a good job and could easily have led us into Super League. He had the backing of the players and we all knew what a great coach he was.

For me, Brian's departure meant an awful end to a season that had promised so much. There was now a feeling we just wanted to get that season over and get Super League started. After Brian left, we lost our last four games of the old league season against St Helens, Workington, Halifax and Oldham, which may have been the straw that broke the camel's back as far as Clive was concerned. Those results ensured the club would make a new start in the coaching department.

When Clive didn't get the job, Alex Murphy was appointed as rugby football executive at Warrington, alongside John Dorahy, the former Wigan coach, and Rob Tew. Clive was pretty devastated by the decision, telling *The Guardian*: 'I am gutted, and will have to sit down and discuss my future with the club.'

The new regime arrived at Warrington, now renamed the Warrington Wolves, and we started pretty well. Our first Super League game under the new management was at Leeds. We beat them 22–18 and everything was pretty sweet.

But the more the season went on the more I distrusted the regime, although I thought that Rob Tew, the assistant coach who looked after the A team, was an excellent coach and a very honest man. I did have run-ins with John Dorahy and Alex Murphy and initially I'd lumped Rob in with those two but I have to admit I completely misread him. When I began to have problems with the club I remember being late for training with the A team one time after getting stuck in traffic. That was the kind of excuse they were looking for to suspend me but he said, 'Don't worry about it,' and sat me down and we chatted about my future, where I was going, what I wanted to do and the best ways to get there.

Warrington became a very unhappy place for me. I certainly wasn't enjoying my rugby any more, and I felt it was a time to move on. I had a full year under the new regime, who said things would get better. However, I didn't agree with some of the things they were doing with other players.

I don't think there was any one incident but I thought they treated players disrespectfully. Brian Johnson always had the ultimate respect of all his players. He demanded respect and got it because of the way he was with everyone. Clive was the same. It was always a friendly, family club which was going in a great direction and the players wanted to be there but with the new regime everything changed, there was a ruthless streak. I felt John Dorahy and Alex Murphy came in with reputations and expected everyone to accept everything they said. They didn't seem to bother about the kids. Eventually, I left, Paul Sculthorpe left and it became a place where players didn't want to be.

I always believed the club was under financial pressure at the time and in later years that was confirmed, although they were doing all they could to hide the true state of affairs. Looking back,

I think Alex Murphy was brought in to shake up the club. He must have been told to come in and try and make money.

Transfer fees were one way of relieving the financial pressure. I think a couple of players were earmarked to make that money and I was one of them. They saw me as the person they could get the most for, so it seemed to me that their idea was to make things a little bit difficult for me so I'd ask for a transfer. Then they could put it out that I'd asked to leave with the club being seen as victims. That's how it turned out.

Of course nobody knew that: they just saw it as me asking for a transfer but that wasn't the case. I was 19 and I'd got on the Great Britain tour, so it wasn't hurting my international chances being at Warrington and I didn't feel that I needed to go.

I was moved around the team: one minute I was full-back, then centre, stand-off, scrum-half and even loose forward. I thought, 'What's going on? I can't have this for the rest of my career. I'm going to have to move on.' They were trying to sell me to rugby union because that's where they could get the most money, but I didn't want to go at that time of my career.

Warrington told me at one stage, 'You can go, but you can go to Wales,' as they had done a deal with Wales and Terry Cobner. Terry and Albert Francis from Cardiff came up to see me and offered me more money than I'd get anywhere else. I'd already had that offer earlier in my career but at this stage I still had so much more I wanted to achieve in rugby league. I had only made my debut in league a few years before and wasn't ready to go to rugby union, but it kept going back and forth for weeks and months. They were both nice guys and very understanding but Warrington were trying to force me into doing something I didn't want to do.

If the club had sat me down and said, 'Iestyn, we have some financial problems and we need to sell you,' I would have understood and if the deal was right for me I would have signed it. Surely the best thing would have been to keep me in the first team and put me in the shop window for other clubs to see me.

It did turn nasty towards the end and I thought that was unnecessary.

I said I wanted to move to another rugby league club and their reply was, 'You won't play for five years, that's what you've got on your contract. You won't move anywhere, we'll put you in the A team.' I had been told I'd never play for Warrington again and that I'd be left to rot in the A team.

Warrington was a players' club, a very together club but when the new regime came in, from the players' point of view the club lost its identity. They brought a lot of players in who didn't fit into the team and towards the end of the first Super League season I knew I had to leave.

I eventually told them it wasn't working and I wanted a transfer. From then on everything changed – it all turned sour. The club's response to my request was to put an utterly ridiculous £1.35 million price tag on my head. Warrington must have known they were never going to get anyone to pay that for me but still they asked for it and that fee ensured that I was, in effect, off limits to every club, whether union or league.

I was stunned when the club issued the following statement, 'After careful consideration the club have decided that Iestyn Harris will not be included in the team for the remaining three matches of the Super League season.

'This decision was arrived at after taking into account the fact Iestyn requested a transfer, there are doubts over his fitness and we need to build a team to go forward without him.'

I was disappointed to be told I couldn't play in those final three games. I had good friends at the club and just because I was on the transfer list it shouldn't have precluded me from playing. I was then told I could play but it would be in the A team, under Rob Tew, and I received a letter from Warrington chief executive John Smith which said,

We feel that having made your decision to move on we cannot allow this to disrupt the rest of the team who are fighting hard to regain fourth spot in the Super League.

The constant uncertainty and speculation is detrimental to performance and your obvious unhappiness is not having a positive effect on the other team members. To avoid any further friction we wish you to train at home until advised otherwise.

Everyone had a month off at the end of the season and when we went back in October to prepare for the next one, there were a group of about eight players either out of contract or in negotiations with the club. We all went into a mini-training group which wasn't allowed to train with the rest of the squad. We were told we had to train at the ridiculous time of four in the morning, because the club could demand that we trained when they told us to train. In their letter the club had talked about 'friction', but as far as I was concerned there wasn't any friction. I was operating under a standard rugby league contract which basically allowed them to do anything they wanted. Thank goodness things have changed. I don't think a club could get away with treating anyone that way these days.

The training times changed – some days it would be at 4 a.m. and other days later. Sometimes the team would be training in and around the pitch while our group just did laps. We would run around the edge while they were in the middle.

I think they were trying to force players from our group to either sign up again or leave. I'm not saying it was specifically against me but I don't know what they were trying to achieve. I had put in a transfer request but the club never sat down and told me what they wanted me to do.

One of the players in dispute with the club was Paul Cullen, who is now the coach at Warrington. I remember Paul saying to me: 'Don't let anybody break you. If you're running round, have a smile on your face and be as upbeat as you can. You can be as miserable as you like at home but when you're in public don't show anybody how you're feeling.' I did that right the way through and I think that frustrated them more than anything. They expected me to say, 'OK, I'll go to rugby union, just get me out of here.' But I wanted to stay in league and needed to go to the right place.

Gradually, the training group dwindled down as some signed and others left. It ended up with just me and Andy Currier. We would go for runs around the fields, often at bizarre times. As there were two of us we had a bit of a chuckle while we were doing it and we got on pretty well. Andy and I did that for around a month before he finally left to go to London Welsh, leaving me on my own. There was still another eight weeks' pre-season to go, so I spent those eight weeks on my own.

I used to get up at about 3.30 a.m. to be at the club for about 4. I met Becky around this time, so it meant I was getting back from training as she was leaving the house to go to college.

They had me doing all sorts of things, running around the roads and up and down the terraces at the ground. A guy called Phil Chadwick used to wait for me at the club. He would apologise and say he was under orders to make me do this training. They even banned me from the gym, so all I could do was run, either on the roads or up and down the terraces.

It was strange at the time and it is even more bizarre looking back on it. I was losing weight and I just wanted to play. I started the pre-season around 13½ st., which is my natural weight, but when I finally signed for Leeds in April 1997, I was down to 11 st. because of all the running I was doing, probably 7 or 8 miles a day.

I think Warrington wanted me to refuse to train so I would have been breaking my contract and then they could have stopped paying me. But there was no way they were going to break me. I used to come in and smile and get on with it. My hands were tied, but I had to keep training and training under their rules until something happened. I was worried because I knew no one was going to pay £1.35 million for me.

I know many people believed that I put in a transfer request either to get more money or to play rugby union and neither was true. Clearly I had a mortgage to pay so I wasn't keen on a pay cut but if it was the right move for me then I would have considered it.

Training dragged on, but soon it was time for the season to start. It came around with speculation in the press that I would be moving to either St Helens in league or Saracens in union. Saracens did come in with a couple of offers but I think the ludicrous transfer fee prevented anything happening.

During those dark days in the dispute with Warrington there were a number of people who helped me. Iain McCorquodale, who at that time was a coach at Oldham, provided me with help and advice and supervised training sessions for me with Brian Quinlan, one of their players. He had been my deputy head at school and I consider him a real friend. Jimmy Russell once more came to help me with my running skills, just when I needed it most. Along with my family, those people were rocks for me.

People often ask if there was one single event that led to my turmoil at Warrington, but there wasn't. Sure, they were asking me to play in a variety of different positions and I wanted to settle at stand-off but in the end it was the culmination of many things that led to my transfer request. I'm not that petty a person to allow one thing to come between me and my club. You must put fall-outs and arguments to one side. They are no reason to leave a club.

It wasn't even a personal thing with the new regime. I respected Alex Murphy for what he had done in the game and I respected John Dorahy. I thought he was a fantastic player. But after the way they acted, my feelings for them changed. I didn't want to be part of their club.

I did play for Warrington in 1997, despite my career at the club apparently being over. In 1996 they wanted to 'go forward without me' but at the beginning of the 1997 season I was back in the side, so you can see how I became confused. I played a reserve-team game against Leeds early in February and scored a try, then John Dorahy asked me to play against the Sheffield Eagles in the fifth round of the Challenge Cup on 23 February, despite the fact that I was still training on my own. I hadn't trained with the first team, which was bizarre. I was really thrown into the game. I knew some of the calls from the previous season but none of the new ones, so I just had to make do and try my best to pick them up. I came off the bench in the second half to a pretty good reception from the Warrington supporters and I hope I did my bit to get them through, kicking three goals, the last of them two minutes from time.

They picked me the week after, against Salford in the next round of the Cup, and I still wasn't training with the first team. We lost 29–10. Incredibly, the players were great all the way through this period and they gave me loads of good-natured stick when I eventually did get back in the first team. I still got on well with them. They were just laughing at what was happening and taking the mickey, while the coaches were hardly speaking to me.

There was another bizarre twist when I managed to incur a 48-hour suspension for playing in a game of soccer, another incident that was blown out of all proportion. I had always been a bad, but enthusiastic, goalkeeper and enjoyed my five-a-side. My friends were playing football, not an organised game, and I decided to join in.

When I came to training there was a picture of a guy in the local paper with his arms in the air saying, 'I scored a goal against Iestyn Harris,' and I thought, 'Oh my God, what is this?' I knew there would be trouble. They pulled me in and said, 'We hear you played football yesterday?'

'Yes,' I answered, as I didn't think there was anything wrong with that. They suspended me, though, on full pay, until they investigated it.

It was ludicrous. There is nothing in any contract I have signed to say I can't play five-a-side football. I play now and did right the way through my time at Warrington. Of course there are sports I can't play, dangerous sports, but five-a-side doesn't fall into that category. I signed for Leeds soon after, so nothing more was said about it.

One much-needed respite from the awful time I was having at Warrington came in the form of Great Britain's tour to Papua New Guinea, Fiji and New Zealand and then a place in the Great Britain World Nines team. I think I would have gone anywhere on any tour to get away from training on my own at four in the morning, passing the milk floats on my way. However, to get my first Great Britain call-up was magnificent. Phil Larder, the GB coach at the time, said that what was happening between Warrington and myself was nothing to do with him. I was so grateful to be given the chance to play rugby league for Great Britain. This tour saw me make my debut in the Test against Papua New Guinea. At the time it was an unbelievable relief because I had come out of a bizarre situation and jumped into the Great Britain side.

At the end of the first Super League season, in August 1996, Jason Robinson, Gary Connolly and Robbie Paul had all taken short-term contracts to play rugby union, Jason to play for Bath, Gary and Robbie for Harlequins. There was some talk of me joining them and perhaps spending some of the off-season in Wales before the start of the 1997 Super League season. However, if I was going to move to union I wanted to do it properly, not some sort of half-hearted move for three months and then come back. I felt that people may have got the wrong impression of me in union if I had gone for such a short amount of time. I knew I would probably go at some time in my career, so it had to be right.

I don't think those three going to union achieved much. Financially they benefited but it was a bit of a sideshow and I don't think it achieved much for either code. It was symptomatic of the way rugby union handled their manic rush towards professionalism. A lot of things happened in those early years after the game went open in 1995 that would never be repeated.

Following my return from that GB tour and after my two

appearances for Warrington, it was soon time for a new chapter in my life. Little did I know at the time what an incredible chapter it was going to be.

St Helens were close to putting together a deal to take me from Warrington and I think I'd have agreed to join them had it all come together. I think they had offered £300,000 around January time. I had spoken to them a number of times and said I would be more than happy to join them if something could be done on the transfer fee side. But they couldn't manage the fee that Warrington were asking for me, so we never got any further. I had a number of friends at St Helens but it was just one of those things and I just had to get on with it. That's part of life as a professional rugby player.

The choice to go to Leeds over St Helens was never really mine. It was up to them to match Warrington's valuation of me before I got involved. My transfer saga just dragged on and on. Each day it seemed a different scenario was being played out in the press. However, at the start of April it was all over and I put pen to paper with the Leeds Rhinos, a deal that was sorted out in three or four days.

As I've always said, my motivation for leaving a club has never been money and this time it definitely wasn't. I had the chance to play union but turned it down and when I finally ended my nightmare time at Warrington I didn't even receive a pay rise! I was earning £75,000 a year at Warrington which was exactly the same as I was to be paid by Leeds. I don't think anyone moves in league because they are being offered much better money – teams tend to offer players similar sorts of wage. It may happen in football but not in rugby. There had always been talk about me going to Leeds but I thought it was just hearsay. I think that's how Leeds have always worked – they sit back and come in at the last minute.

They drove a hard bargain with Warrington but I don't blame them for that. They are a business, after all, and it is up to them to sign players for as little money as they can.

My agent at the time rang me to say there was a deal on the table and Gary Hetherington, the chief executive at Leeds, rang me to see if I was interested in going to Headingley. He said they could do the deal and he'd talk personal terms. I remember that I took about five minutes to agree to make the move from Warrington and about ten minutes to agree the personal terms with Gary.

Leeds agreed to pay Warrington £325,000, which showed how ludicrous their earlier price tag of £1.35 million was. The package rose to £350,000 with Daniel Sculthorpe, an Academy prop, moving from Headingley to Wilderspool. This was second in money-only terms to the £440,000 Wigan paid Widnes for Martin Offiah in 1992.

Relief was my main reaction after I signed for Leeds, relief that my nine-month nightmare was over. I was always optimistic, even in the darkest days, that a deal to take me away from Warrington would be done. I had to believe it was just a question of when, not if.

There was never a problem with the players at Warrington. I still get booed when I go back there but today it is a completely different place to what it was back in 1996. The whole regime has changed. The coaches have changed and the chairman has gone. When I think of Warrington now, I look back on my days with enjoyment. I joined as a wide-eyed 15 year old and had a good time. I made some great friends, enjoyed the social side and enjoyed my rugby.

I was now looking forward to a new club and new players. I knew the Leeds coach Dean Bell quite well. He had played for Wigan for many years and he was a guy I had a lot of respect for. I spoke to him just before I signed. He was very welcoming but I didn't talk to him about my position in the side. I certainly didn't make demands before I put pen to paper.

Dean said that as long as the deal could be done he'd put me on the bench the following day, against Wigan. He was keen to give me a run out and I was lucky to be able to do the team run, the last ball session before the game, before the press conference announcing my arrival at Leeds. My position wasn't really an issue, the most important thing was that I just wanted to be a part of a team again.

Lewis Jones, a legend who once cost Leeds a record transfer fee, was at Headingley to greet me on the day I was introduced to the Leeds public at that press conference. I'd never met him before but obviously I had heard of him and it was great to see him.

Some people may have thought that a transfer fee that size would hang around my neck. But, despite how big it was, I had to put it to one side. After the way it ended at Warrington what was important to me was playing. The size of the fee never really became an issue. I didn't feel under pressure because of it and 1997 was a learning time for the Leeds club. It was accepted that it was a building year and that helped me settle in.

I knew a few of the Leeds players, including prop Barrie McDermott, who's from Oldham and has been a great friend to me over the years. I used to travel over to Leeds with Barrie and I also struck up a great friendship with winger Paul Sterling.

I never had a problem in that dressing-room – they took to me very well. That says a lot for those Leeds boys because they could easily have resented me and my huge transfer fee.

Graham Holroyd was their stand-off at the time and my main rival for the jersey but even Graham was great and I became good friends with him. He had every reason to be cold towards me, but Graham made a big effort and never made it awkward. I think that's the general attitude in rugby – people treat you with respect. Graham certainly did and I thank him for that.

Following the nightmare of my last few months at Warrington I was still around two stones below my ideal weight, but after a fee like that, Leeds were only going to do one thing and that was get me playing as quickly as possible. I signed on Thursday, 3 April, and Dean Bell was as good as his word: I was in the squad for the Super League match on the Friday against the Wigan Warriors at Headingley!

That first game was a big disappointment as we lost 17–16, a late Andrew Farrell drop goal proving decisive. I did have some success though and it was a relief, as I wanted to make a good impression. With my first touch I wrong-footed Terry O'Connor and Tony Smith and sent Phil Hassan in for a try, before kicking the conversion, which settled my nerves. I was able to make a few more breaks and we took it to them that night, although in those days Wigan were a better organised side and just had the edge on us. They had the structure in the team to settle for the drop-goal winner.

That game set the trend for the rest of the year. We had the right flair but we didn't have the structure to win the big games and I think that is something we built on over the years.

I had two or three decent performances in my first few games and I think that released the pressure a little bit. This was important, especially at Leeds, as the fans can be a little fickle at times. I remember Keith Senior coming in 1999 and he started poorly. He struggled to score and the fans were booing him. It took him time to win them over but he did. I think I played those first two or three games on adrenaline as I was far from ready from a conditioning point of view. My weight was low and it took me a year to get it back up to where I wanted it.

After the first loss to Wigan things took a huge turn for the better as we inflicted the first defeat of the season on St Helens, the other club that almost signed me, at Headingley. This was another difficult game for me because before signing for Leeds I had been linked with St Helens for probably six months. At the time they were Challenge Cup holders and Super League champions and a major force in the game, so they would have turned up at Headingley expecting to win.

Once again things went well. In the first half we were straight out of the blocks and I managed to contribute, with my kicking, to a 12–8 half-time lead. I also set up a try for Paul Sterling.

It looked as though the Saints would snatch this one after a Bobbie Goulding try in the 79th minute made it 13–12 to us with the conversion to come. It was just five yards to the side of the posts and we presumed we had lost as Bobbie doesn't miss those sort of kicks, but the ball hit the left upright and we were home, thanks to the drop goal I had managed to land a few minutes before. The whole ground erupted as if we had won at Wembley. It was just one league game but it meant so much at the time because we felt like we were building and to beat St Helens was a massive building block.

It was inevitable that I would come up against Warrington and we beat them 50–12 at Headingley towards the end of May. I had reservations about going back to Wilderspool for the return fixture on 11 July but I knew it was better to get it over with. There was never any question of me ducking the game. I pulled up in the coach and saw people outside whom I had known since I was 15.

One of the first people I saw when I arrived at the ground was Evelyn, who sold the Golden Gamble tickets. I had been friends with her for five or six years. She was a lovely lady and it was great to see her and so many other people with whom I had grown up.

Although things went wrong for me at Warrington towards the end, it couldn't affect the love I had for the club and many of the people who were the heart and soul of it. Those people were great and I think it settled my nerves to see them again.

I nearly went in the home dressing-room by mistake, perhaps showing how nervous I was. We got changed and went out and the crowd were quite hostile towards me but it wasn't too bad. Of course I expected it but we got on top early and I think that made a big difference as it quietened them down. We won the game, I kicked five goals from five attempts and set up two of Leeds' tries, though under severe pressure at times. Although it was inevitable that the crowd would get on my back, the players were great. There were a few that I didn't know, faces that had changed since I was there, who were trying to have a dig. But the ones I had played with were fine – they knew what had happened.

Paul Cullen had just joined in a coaching capacity and he was great too. I went into the bar afterwards to have a drink and didn't have any problems. There was never really a problem between me and the people in the club. It was the hierarchy who had the problem and I believed they never understood the club.

The big games kept coming that season and soon we were heading south to play in the 1997 World Club Challenge. This proved to be a one-off competition where the twelve British Super League clubs were pitted against the ten from the Australian competition. Initially the teams were divided into two pools and we were in Group B with the North Queensland Cowboys and the Adelaide Rams. It was always going to be very difficult for the British teams because the British game was still building at that time and this competition was perhaps a year too early. They were asking teams who just weren't ready to go to Australia and play their top sides. There were some heavy defeats as the English teams were unable to perform against the Australians. We did pretty well in most of our games but it was just too much too soon.

With the advent of Super League many people wanted to make the competition an annual event but I think that was and is totally unrealistic. It was never going to work and if they had to do it, it should have been done as a mini tournament, with maybe four teams from both countries. It was great for the players, of course, as teams like Oldham and Halifax went Down Under. They were never going to compete against the Australian sides but the players made sure they had a pretty good time! The World Club Challenge is now an annual game between the Super League championship and the champions of the National Rugby League in Australia.

Although I enjoyed my first year at Leeds, in my heart I know I didn't perform in the way I would have liked. We had just over half a season left when I joined them and although I played in every game, I felt I was just off the pace. It took me that year to bed myself back into the game.

A back injury kept me out of the Great Britain v Australia series at the end of that season. I think the injury came from playing when I was underweight for so long. My back was very painful and I needed to rest it, which was definitely the right decision.

I couldn't wait to get back to Super League and my first full season for the Leeds Rhinos. I had put on a couple of stones over the year and was getting near to my playing weight, so that rest was just what I needed to get myself ready for the 1998 season.

No sooner had we returned for pre-season training at Leeds than Dean Bell was on his way out, to be replaced by Australian Graham Murray as head coach. Dean went straight into coaching from playing and perhaps you need to do the groundwork before you can take on such a big job as the Leeds Rhinos. I thought Dean did well but perhaps lacked the experience that you get by coaching Academies and A teams before moving up to the first team. Dean subsequently took up a role as head of youth development at the club.

Graham Murray had been coaching in Australia and he was the perfect man for the club. He was direct, focused on what he wanted and had great man-management skills. He set the tone for the year with his pre-season work. I got on very well with Graham and with Edgar Curtis, the fitness coach, who got everyone physically ready. Graham became the catalyst for a new regime at Headingley and in his first press conference he set out his stall for the way he wanted us to play. 'There's a good foundation here,' he said, 'but it's a bit more of an attractive style of football that I'd like to play. There's a balance to be struck. Winning is the bottom line but we are in the entertainment business and we've got to give people a match worth watching.'

I remember there was a great atmosphere at that time and a healthy desire at the club. Graham brought a really good focus to Headingley and we had the feeling we were on the verge of something big. Graham also brought in some good players from Australia, Brad Godden and Marc Glanville, and at that stage we had the foundations of a very good team.

We lost early on in the Challenge Cup to Castleford 15–12,

which at the time was hard to take. However, in the long run, that defeat perhaps helped us. There was still about six weeks to the start of the Super League season so it gave us extra time to get things right and, come the first game, we kicked off with a bang.

As I have already mentioned, I was disappointed with my first season at Leeds, so I was determined to put things right in the second season. I knew I owed it to myself.

I did a lot of work with Edgar and he proved to be a fantastic fitness coach, giving me every chance to succeed in that campaign. Working with him gave me confidence and I felt I was in good shape again.

Graham, who had experience from all around the world, had only been at Headingley a month when he made his first big decision – to make me captain. Gary Mercer, who led the season before, had left. There was a lot of experience in the side and I thought he would hand the role to either Tony Kemp or Marc Glanville. Graham was a very astute man and he didn't make his decision immediately. He let everyone train and wonder. Pre-season was really good and I had trained well. After a while he pulled me to one side to see if I was interested and I jumped at the chance.

I'd never even thought about being skipper and it certainly wasn't something I had expected, although when it came I regarded it as a huge honour. It was a big surprise as I was still only 20 and hadn't been at the club very long. I had done a little bit of captaincy at Warrington but nothing official before, even in my amateur days. Graham said that he felt I could take the club forward in the right way. He talked about my attitude in training and gave me a few tips about what he thought a captain should be. He wanted his captain to be selfless and do things for the team first. They might not always be the things which were best for me personally, but he said if I did that it would go well. I hope I always made an effort as captain to carry out that philosophy.

We went up to Newcastle for a fitness weekend and then we went to an Army camp, which at the time was horrendous but,

My granddad, captain of the Newbridge rugby union team, in 1942.

Father and son: my dad and granddad
around 1946.

My dad, following in the family
rugby tradition, around 1947.

My mum had a sense of humour when it came to dress sense.

Me and my granddad showing off our Welsh rugby league caps.

Down but not out: our lap around Old Trafford after our loss to England in the '95 World Cup.

Inset: Having fun: me and my half-back partner Bobby Goulding on tour in '96 with Great Britain. (both © Andrew Varley)

A great day: plate success with Wales in Fiji in the world 10-a-side competition.
(© Andrew Varley)

Practice time: me and my dad putting some work in on my goalkicking (© Andrew Varley)

You beauty! Lifting the Challenge Cup with Leeds Rhinos in 1999. (© Andrew Varley)

Plastered in make-up doing a photo shoot for my sponsors Tissot! (© Tissot)

The Rugby League
World Cup, 2000.
(© Cleva)

The first of three: on my way to the line for my first try against Glasgow on my
full debut for Cardiff at the Arms Park.

Proud as punch: me and my mate Anthony Sullivan
picking up our caps for the Welsh Rugby Union.

Wales v. Ireland in the 2003 Six Nations. (© Cleva)

Becky and me on our wedding day, June 2003. (© Ronald Turner)

Me, Becky and Catrin with Mum, Dad, Rhiain, Dave, Dewi and Emrys. (© Ronald Turner)

Becky and Catrin, my beautiful wife and daughter.

Holiday time: me and Catrin having a dip in the Turks and Caicos Islands.

looking back, the trip did the side a lot of good. We were running around in mud in the freezing cold but it helped build the team spirit.

That team spirit took us through our first game, which was a 30–8 win over my old club Warrington. Matches against them were now just another game. They had a good side. Unfortunately I didn't finish the match, going off with a twisted knee, but perhaps the most important victory came in the next game against our fierce rivals, Bradford.

I came back from that injury and managed to score a hat-trick in our 26–6 win at Odsal. This was a big game for us, one we had focused on throughout pre-season.

The victory ended Leeds' six-match losing run against our big West Yorkshire rivals. It was in many ways a bizarre day. I'll never forget the weather conditions we had to overcome. We went out for the warm-up and it was sunny, then it rained before the hail stones began to fall. There was even some snow before it became sunny again! But as in the game against Warrington, our defence was brutal. I'm not sure if Bradford were as focused as we were but we really took it to them.

The hat-trick and the man of the match award meant it was a good day for me and more importantly an excellent day for the club. That win made us believe we could really do something in this competition, leaving us alongside Halifax, Wigan and Hull as the only sides with 100 per cent records after the opening two rounds.

There were a few skirmishes in the game with Bradford which ended with 11 men on each side. Second row Sonny Nickle was sent off seven minutes from the end after fighting with our centre Richie Blackmore, who was sent to the sin bin. Two minutes later, Stuart Spruce (Bradford) and Francis Cummins (Leeds) joined Blackmore in the bin after trading punches in another flare-up.

That was the game where we started to believe we were on the verge of something big. If you looked around the Leeds side at that time there were a lot of good, dedicated players. We were a very physical side and the two Australians who came in, Brad and Marc, were great for us. They didn't arrive with massive reputations but those two stamped their authority on the team and seemed to give everyone else a lift. Bradford didn't like it. They had been really dominant over Leeds for some time and now Leeds were coming onto their patch and winning and they knew it wasn't a lucky result. It was a convincing victory, in which we were physically dominant.

I don't believe we were over the top but we resolved to make sure nobody was going to take liberties with us in this season. It wasn't a conscious decision to change our image but there's no doubt we became a team that wasn't prepared to back down.

As we had such a physical side we had set a goal of having the most brutal defence in the league. Our two front rowers, Anthony Farrell and Darren Fleary, set the tone for the whole side. They'd be the ones who came up with the big hits and we all followed them. We were just a very physical side right the way through from one to thirteen.

Our mental approach to Super League was also very strong and we wouldn't be knocked off course. We must have been doing something right because we were unbeaten in our first four matches, the club's best start to a season for ten years.

We finished the season second in the table to Wigan but a new system had been introduced which meant that the team finishing top of the league weren't automatically crowned champions. Instead, the top five teams played off against each other, although the higher-placed club in each match had home advantage apart from the final which was played at Old Trafford.

The top club had a bye in the first stage and then needed only one win to take them into the final. We won our qualifying play-off 13–6 against Halifax, who had finished third and then played the Wigan Warriors at Central Park in the qualifying semi-final. They won 17–4 to go straight into the final but we had another chance. St Helens, who had finished fourth, had beaten Halifax 37–30 to set up a meeting with us in the final eliminator at

Headingley. Whoever won would go to Old Trafford to face Wigan.

We put on a great display, beating them 44–16 and scoring seven tries, winger Francis Cummins collecting a hat-trick. After that game, Graham said, 'To blow Saints away like that shows we are running into good form at the right time. It was a very professional performance. Now we are looking forward to another Wigan battle.'

Over the year, we had beaten Wigan twice in our Super League encounters and only lost to them in the play-off game. There was a great determination to bring a trophy back to Headingley as it had been so long since they'd won anything.

In that first-ever Grand Final, there was absolutely nothing between the teams. We made a few breaks early on and then Richie Blackmore scored, but just before half-time they took the lead. A guy called Jason Robinson danced along the line, shot through a gap which simply wasn't there and scored under the posts. That try absolutely crushed us as there was nothing on. He was the only one who could have got through that gap. Andy Farrell added the conversion to make it 6–4 at half-time and in a very tight second half he kicked two penalties to give them a 10–4 victory.

There was a huge feeling of frustration in the club after that defeat as we not only felt we were the best team in the competition but we were also the most physical. We'd beaten everyone in the league right the way through and we felt we'd let ourselves down in those two games against Wigan. It's very frustrating and very deflating to lose when you know you could have won.

As the pain of the defeat faded, there was certainly a feeling of pride in the squad about what we had achieved. The determination was there to make sure we never had that feeling again. We got together on the Sunday after the Grand Final to have a drink and reflected on how well we had done over the year. Of course we were disappointed but crucially for our future success no one at the Rhinos was prepared to accept second best. It was important we acknowledged the position we had risen to in Super League and the progress we had made but we weren't happy with anything else but trophies. We stamped our authority on Super League and the feeling in the squad was that we were going to work even harder in the pre-season and come back and do it again. It was disappointing but perhaps the defeat in the Grand Final gave us more focus.

I think Wigan's winning mentality and the success they'd had before was significant in the way they were able to close out games. There is nothing to beat a winning mentality, one that makes you believe you are never beaten. So often you see sides losing their first final before coming back and winning.

On a personal level I was quite proud because I had been named Man of Steel which is rugby league's top individual award. I also won the Super League's Players' Player of the Year award and the Rugby League Writers' Association Player of the Year trophy.

The following year the promise that the Leeds team had shown came through. I think it was destiny that we drew Wigan in our first game of 1999, which was the fourth round of the Challenge Cup. Again we trained well in the off-season and everyone was looking good. We were soon 6–0 up and cruising when Barrie McDermott was sent off, not for a reckless challenge, but a loose arm which caught the Wigan forward Simon Haughton. I thought Barrie was very unlucky to go off for that challenge but we then faced the prospect of surviving for 60 minutes with 12 men, a real mountain. Normally it would be nigh-on impossible to compete against a side like Wigan with 12 men but we came in at half-time and said there would be no excuses. There was a resolve in the team that we were going to do it. In the end we won convincingly 28–18.

Beating Wigan so soon after losing to them in that Grand Final and particularly after losing Barrie, made everyone believe this was the season when we would win our silverware, a feeling which turned into reality when we won the Challenge Cup. Even now it's hard to express in words my joy and pride at being captain on that great day at Wembley and lifting the cup in front of those magnificent fans.

We drew some big sides in the run-up. After beating Wigan, St Helens were up next at home and we'd said all year there was no way we were going to lose at home. It was a tough game but we were always going to win it and a 24–16 victory took us another step on the road to Wembley. However, the road nearly ended in the quarter-finals at Widnes who were then in the First Division. There seemed to be a feeling we were always going to win the game but at half-time we were only 12–10 ahead and hardly cruising! Then a teenager called Kevin Sinfield, just out of the Academy, came off the bench and changed the game. He was the new kid on the block and he created a couple of tries out of nothing to kick-start us. We went on to turn the game around and Kevin had kicked off his career for Leeds.

We eventually made it to Wembley, beating Bradford in the semis, at Huddersfield. We went 10–0 down and the Twin Towers seemed a million miles away as they looked in complete control. We pulled it back to 10–8 at half-time and then proceeded to turn in the best 40 minutes of our cup run. A try from Francis Cummins just after half-time began the revival and after I scored under the sticks we killed the game off and began our plans for the Challenge Cup final. To beat Bradford in a major semi-final was a good feeling and it meant so much to the club and the group of players.

It was a great, great day for the players and supporters and the celebrations after that semi were massive. We had a quiet night after the game and then, as we had a week off, we met up the next day and had a good drink and a barbecue at the club to finish off. We had worked so hard and now it was time to enjoy each other's company, kick back and start the build-up for the final. I spent a lot of time that night with my long-time mate Barrie McDermott and I remember speaking to Kevin Sinfield, who was from Oldham as well.

Barrie and I used to travel together to training and on those journeys we got to know each other very well. Everyone portrays Barrie as this rough, tough guy but he's not at all like that. He is mild-mannered and great to be around. Barrie was very worried because he'd got sent off against Wigan at the start of our cup run and picked up a big ban. He missed the St Helens game, but played against Widnes and Bradford. He was concerned he was going to miss the whole run so the relief when he helped us to get to Wembley was massive for him. I was delighted to see him come through that period because I still don't believe his tackle against Wigan deserved a red card.

When the final whistle blew after the semi-final win I immediately looked for Barrie. He was so relieved because I knew he would blame himself if we hadn't made it. I think Graham Murray made him aware that he had to do something for the team to make up for his sending off and, to be fair, he did, playing really well in the other games. No one would ever have blamed Barrie if we hadn't made it in 1999 (well, I wouldn't have), but then, like most professional players, he is always his own biggest critic.

Our 1998 final turned out to be just a taster of what was to come in 1999, and stood us in great stead for our walk up Wembley Way. This Challenge Cup was extra special as it was the last final at Wembley before it was torn down and rebuilt. Not long after Wales had beaten England in the Five Nations, we arrived to take on the London Broncos.

I remember we stayed in a country hotel near Watford, about 25 miles from London. We were there from Wednesday onwards and had a really good build-up. We trained in the grounds of Eton College and used all of Eton's facilities, which were obviously excellent, before going down to Wembley the day before the match for a run-out. The week built up really nicely as we were in our own little cocoon.

The final turned out to be one of the most memorable days not only in my life but in the life of the Leeds Rhinos. It was another great milestone in what had already been an incredible career in rugby league for me.

Before the game I remember thinking that, surprisingly, we were all really calm, walking around the pitch with our suits on, taking in the atmosphere of a fantastic day for everyone involved. It was magnificent driving into Wembley. There were thousands and thousands of people outside cheering us on and that gave us a huge lift. I'll never forget the journey to that famous ground.

Our opponents were the London Broncos and although we knew we had the beating of them from our games in Super League, we still had to go out and do it. However, once again we were out of the blocks slowly. Looking back, perhaps our poor start was caused by overconfidence and maybe we were all enjoying the day too much to focus on the job in front of us. It was very hot, about 80 to 85 degrees on the pitch, and before we knew what was happening the 8–1 outsiders had scored two tries and were 10–0 up.

We couldn't believe that Wembley was going to see another massive shock. Twelve months earlier, the Sheffield Eagles caused one of the biggest ever Challenge Cup final upsets by beating Wigan and the neutrals must have thought another one was on the cards. I remember looking around and thinking this was not the Leeds Rhinos team I knew. I thought London hadn't read the script or they had a different script to the one we were given! We were dropping balls and missing tackles, which is something we hadn't done all season. Martin Offiah had scored a long-range try, against a side that prided itself on its aggressive, physical presence on the pitch.

But that all changed as we approached half-time. We created two really quick tries out of nothing to go in 12–10 ahead. Winger Leroy Rivett got the first and the second came deep in first-half injury time when prop Darren Fleary broke through deep and fed centre Brad Godden, who swapped passes with Lee Jackson before going under the posts.

We all knew there was no way we should be up after the half

we'd endured, so the focus in the dressing-room was to gee the boys up and get them switched on so we could physically start to dominate the second half. Graham Murray calmed everyone down and emphasised that we must approach the second half as if it was just another game. We needed to forget we were in the final and treat it like a normal Super League encounter. We knew we hadn't performed well and there was a feeling that we couldn't perform that badly again in the second half. Effectively, we had to start the game again.

Brad Godden was crucial in getting us back into it, as was Barrie McDermott. I remember him roaring through some Broncos tackles early in the second half to score a try that made us believe we were on our way to victory. Everything clicked in that second half with a series of tries. We got on a roll and they couldn't stop us. We then started to enjoy the game and when you can relax and do that you are bound to win.

As a team we were very aware of what that day meant to the people of Leeds and it was a big factor in why we weren't prepared to come away from Wembley without the Challenge Cup. More than 30,000 of them made the journey from Yorkshire and we wanted to deliver for them. There was a lot of pressure on the club, as it had been 21 years since they had won a trophy. This group of players had only been together for two seasons but we still felt the pressure and I think for the fans it was as much of a relief as anything else.

Leeds had made a lot of finals but they always had Wigan, who had dominated the game for so long, as their rivals. Now today was our day. We went on to record the highest winning total of all time and the biggest winning margin in our 52–16 victory.

I was a very proud captain on the day, kicking eight goals to equal Cyril Kellett's record for Featherstone Rovers against Bradford in 1973. I tried with all my might to make that walk up those Wembley steps last forever and I can still remember the way it felt to lift that cup and turn round to our supporters. It is at those times you try and make time stand still to make the moment last.

Graham Murray said, 'We've put Leeds back on the map. The club is stronger for my being here. The quality of the team was always there, it just needed someone to bring it out, and I was glad I did it.'

Our match-winner was Leroy Rivett, who was 22, and became the first player in history to score four tries in a final. It was a huge day for him. He picked up the Lance Todd trophy, and a cheque for £10,000, after being named man of the match. Although he had been playing well before we got to Wembley he was still relatively unknown and that game put him on another level. Unfortunately he didn't handle his instant fame too well. I really felt for Leroy because the fame and pressure not only came quickly but it came from nowhere. One company said if he scored three tries at Wembley they would give him a Ferrari for a week, which they did. So there was Leroy turning up to training in a Ferrari, drawing everyone's admiration. However, during that week he wrote it off. No one really knew how it happened but the whole thing ended up in court. That one game, the best day of his rugby life, also destroyed his career.

It didn't really sink in at the time that our Challenge Cup final would be the last one at Wembley for some time as it was being rebuilt. But what did sink in was that it was Wembley. The biggest venue in rugby and the goal of so many players, it was a stadium every rugby league player wanted to play at and, on reflection, the fact that we would be the last ones to do it was even better. I had watched Wales beat England there in the Five Nations, which included Scott Gibbs' amazing last-minute try. So, on a personal level, to follow him and that team was magnificent. It was such a special place to be and the feeling running out there will stay with me forever. The Tannoy blasted out Tina Turner's 'Simply the Best' on a day I never wanted to end. The team for that unforgettable day at Wembley was: Iestyn Harris; Leroy Rivett, Richie Blackmore, Brad Godden, Francis Cummins; Daryl Powell, Ryan Sheridan; Darren Fleary, Terry Newton, Barrie McDermott, Adrian Morley, Anthony Farrell,

Marc Glanville. Subs: Lee Jackson, Jamie Mathiou, Andy Hay, Marcus St Hilaire.

After that epic occasion, we all went back to the hotel for a big function where our wives and girlfriends could join us along with the directors and staff. Basically, it was everyone involved in the club enjoying each other's company and celebrating our victory. The day after, we drove back to the city where we had an open-top bus waiting for us. We got on around 1 p.m. and went down the main street in Leeds. I remember at the start there weren't that many people around, just a few dotted about, and we were a little disappointed. But that all changed when the bus turned into Headingley where there were about 40,000 people. That was yet another unforgettable experience for me and the team. We were all on top and it was a carnival atmosphere in the sun.

Everyone was introduced, held the trophy up and we did all we could to go round and meet everyone who was at the ground. From there we went into the changing-rooms and to the bar. There's only one way in and one way out of the changing-rooms. From there it's about 400 yards to the bar and I remember it taking me about four and a half hours to make that journey. It was an enjoyable but very long day.

The trip to Wembley had been a great family day for me. Mum, Dad, my sister (of course) and Becky made the journey to London. My grandfather was a little too old to make it, unfortunately, but I made sure I went to see him the week after with my medal.

It was a strange week because we played on the Saturday, celebrated on the Sunday but still had to come back into the club on the Monday as we had a game on Tuesday. The Challenge Cup final was played on 1 May, so we had over half the Super League season still to go.

It is plainly ridiculous to ask a team to play in a cup final on a Saturday and then take on a high-intensity league game a few days later! Thankfully they don't do that any more. The club tried to get the game postponed but to no avail. Suffice it to say we weren't in exactly great shape for that Tuesday game against St Helens. We had beaten them on the way to Wembley and then we were being asked to go there and win again. I was on the bench and there were a few other injuries but the whole team were feeling a bit rough from the celebrations.

I was told to warm up with a view to coming on but during the time I was warming up they scored three tries and a new message was sent over to me: 'Don't worry, sit down again.' Surprise, surprise, we got hammered 62–18 but we did make up for it a few years later when St Helens made it to the final and then had to play us within days. We put 70 points on them.

It turned out to be a really bizarre year because when we won the cup everything was fantastic. I thought we had the best team in Super League. After the defeat by Saints, we went on a 13-match unbeaten run and we were playing some great stuff. But midway through the season Graham Murray pulled me in and said he was going to go back to Australia at the end of the year, I think one of his parents was ill and he'd been offered a job there. He'd said that he wanted to move back to be near his family and of course we all understood his decision. It was disappointing, which was a compliment to him and what he'd done at Headingley.

I'm not saying that Graham lost interest from then on but I think he lost focus a little bit. He went back to Australia briefly and Damian McGrath took over while he was away. Then Dean Lance, who'd be confirmed as Graham's replacement, came in for a month to oversee things and meet people. It was a little bit silly – he was next year, he shouldn't have been involved this year.

Our winning run came to an end in mid-July at St Helens. Adrian Morley got sent off early in the game and we got a right hammering, losing 28–12. Then it all started to fall apart. There were distractions and our season ended when we lost at home to Castleford in the play-offs.

Still, it felt like Leeds were going places and I wanted to be part of it. I was excited about it and certainly had no intentions of leaving, so in December I signed a new four-year contract.

FIVE

MAKING THE MOVE SOUTH

Ever since I broke into the Warrington first team, in 1993, the rumours about me moving 'south' to rugby union had been circulating. I came close to changing codes in my teenage years but I always felt that the time wasn't right at that stage in my career.

I had always imagined I would end up in union one day but I suppose that feeling became an overwhelming desire during the 2000 Rugby League World Cup, where I was honoured to be captain of Wales. We played our games at the Millennium Stadium and running out to small crowds at that magnificent ground led me to wonder what it would be like to swap my Wales league jersey for one of the union kind and play in front of a full house.

Playing for Wales at rugby league was important to me, of course, but as a young Welsh lad growing up in Oldham I also wanted to feel the passion and desire of a Six Nations Championship or a World Cup in the union code. I wanted to play in front of the Welsh public and show them what I could do. To play with that red shirt on, in front of 70,000 people, was something most young Welshmen dream of and I was no different. I knew deep down that playing for Wales in rugby league I would never have the opportunity to do that.

Rugby union was also very appealing to me. I liked the game and I was ready to take my ambitions to switch codes to the next stage. I suppose a number of circumstances came together to make it possible.

The disappointment at Leeds was a factor in my decision. I certainly wasn't enjoying my rugby at Leeds. After our magnificent Challenge Cup win in 1999 the team was going through a major reconstruction and the frustration I felt was growing week by week. I couldn't see any light at the end of the tunnel. I still believe that at the end of 1999 and the beginning of 2000 we had a Rhinos team that was on the verge of something special. I knew we had the players to kick on but I'm not sure the club itself gave us the backing we needed.

I felt the recruitment system was under par: they simply brought the wrong people in on both the playing and the coaching side. I'm not sure if it was for financial reasons but that influx of new personnel clearly didn't work, as we never followed up our Challenge Cup win. It was frustrating because I believe we'll never know how good the Leeds Rhinos side of the late 1990s could have been. I felt the club, after two glorious years, were back to where they had been and that was disappointing.

That group of players, who won the Challenge Cup in 1999, felt we could rule the roost for a few years once that first trophy was under our belts. So much had come together for us after our disappointment in 1998. We were on the crest of a wave and I believed the club should have been able to kick on. When Graham Murray left, the right decisions should have been made but they weren't. He was replaced by Dean Lance on a very, very low-paid contract. It was his first major coaching position and I don't think he coped well. Leeds is a big, big job. They could have brought better people in but they didn't. Players left and the team fell apart – it was very difficult to take.

Even though we'd had that blip at the end of the 1999 season, we were a very close-knit group and everyone got on. But that all changed. Before the 2000 season, we went to Lanzarote for a week's training camp. Winger Paul Sterling couldn't go as he had a wedding. Sterlo would have been around 33 years of age but he was still a great athlete. I'd seen him score some great tries, which he did regularly. I got on really well with Paul and we were good friends. He was a very clever man, but more of an individual and he worked hard to participate in the team environment. It was difficult for him, he had to push himself to be part of the team atmosphere. I thought he did really well. However, Dean Lance made a decision to cut him from the first-team squad. He felt that he wasn't good enough for the side and hadn't shown commitment because he didn't come to Lanzarote.

He believed that several players felt Paul wasn't pulling his weight, which, as far as I was concerned, wasn't the case. I'd known Paul for years and I knew what a great trainer he was.

Lance made his announcement in Lanzarote when Paul wasn't there and it created a big wave in the team. Suddenly people were talking behind other people's backs. From that moment on, the team was never the same.

It went from a very close-knit squad, who were comfortable with each other, to little cliques. Daryl Powell, Barrie McDermott, Kevin Sinfield and I were comfortable with each other, we had our own little clique. Then there was Francis Cummins, Ryan Sheridan and Keith Senior in another group.

You can't do anything in an atmosphere like that and we just never recovered the team ethos. The players were talking about it at the time; something wasn't right. Graham Murray had always been very insistent about having no 'outsiders' in the squad. His view was, 'We're a team, we work together. If you have any problems come and see me or Damian and we'll sort it out. Don't go talking behind anyone's back, we'll sort it out face to face.'

We went from that to people talking here and there. Even though we were playing reasonably well, it just wasn't right. Something needed to be done and it wasn't. That's one of the main reasons why, when I came back from union, I wasn't willing to go back to Leeds. I didn't feel confident enough given what I'd experienced before.

Our Super League season got off to a disastrous start. We were beaten in our opening game 22–18 by Wakefield at Headingley on 3 March and then lost the next four, which included a 44–10 hammering at Warrington. There were injuries and just no cohesion in the team. It just went from bad to worse. You could feel the club falling apart. In my humble opinion, that came from the top – the right decisions weren't made at the right time. It was so frustrating.

By contrast, we had done well in the defence of the Challenge Cup which kicked off with a win over Featherstone Rovers on 13 February. We then beat St Helens 26–20 and Dewsbury 42–10 to put us in the semi-final where we faced Hull. We still hadn't won a Super League game when we played Hull at the McAlpine Stadium in Huddersfield on 26 March, but we won through to another final with a 28–22 victory.

We only picked up our first Super League win against Huddersfield on 21 April, just a week before our Challenge Cup final appearance against our great rivals, the Bradford Bulls. It was being played at Murrayfield and will probably be remembered for the floods that hit Edinburgh in the run-up to the game and put the match in jeopardy.

Over four feet of water covered the pitch the day before the final but amazingly it was cleared and the match went ahead. It was a strange game, one in which one guy's career was turned upside down in the space of 12 months. Leroy Rivett scored four tries in the 1999 final and became a hero overnight in Leeds. He was fêted at dinners left, right and centre. A year later, at Murrayfield, he dropped two bombs that allowed Bradford to score 12 points and we lost the game. He never recovered from that final – his confidence was shattered.

At half-time we were down 14–2 and had a lot to do to turn it round. Dean Lance came to me and said, 'What should I do?' I said, 'What do you mean?' He replied, 'Should I bring him off or leave him on?' I said, 'To be fair, that's not my decision, I'm in the heat of battle here. I think you should leave him on and let him get through it but that's just my opinion.' He actually left him on and Leroy did come through it OK but Dean Lance should have been making that decision. Even 20 minutes into the game, if he felt it wasn't going right, he should have been aggressive and made the decision, which could have changed the outcome. Dean Lance wasn't keen on making those decisions. Leeds should have known what kind of character he was and what kind of coach he was before he came in.

With just over half an hour left we trailed 20–4, but all credit to the boys they came back and with six minutes remaining Marcus St Hilaire went over for a try, which I converted. There were a few more tries from us in the second half to cut the lead to four points. A penalty from Henry Paul eventually made it 24–18 but in the last minute we put a bomb up and nearly scored. Even though we didn't play particularly well it ended up being a close game.

Bradford scored a couple of tries which on a normal day we wouldn't have conceded but it seemed destined to be their day. Deep down the Leeds players were low on confidence, the feeling was, 'We're here but can we really win it?' Bradford were playing extremely well at the time and the talk in the press was that they were going to win. I didn't think we had the self-belief to win. Henry Paul completed a memorable family double in collecting the man-of-the-match Lance Todd Trophy as his brother and half-back partner Robbie had won it in 1996 when the Bulls lost to St Helens.

Making the move to union was in my mind in 2000 but the time wasn't right as I think it would have created even more waves at Leeds. At the time they just didn't need any more upheaval. I won Player of the Year again in 2000 but I already knew 2001 would be the year I would go to Wales.

Around this time I got my first ever taste of rugby union. I was a member of the Leeds squad, which consisted of both league and union players from the club, that took part in the Middlesex Sevens on 12 August. From the Rhinos there was me, winger Mark Calderwood and a young centre, Chev Walker. We had two training sessions with the Leeds Tykes and their coach Phil Davies who showed us how we should place the ball in the tackle. We talked about keeping the ball alive, as we believed that was the only way we could win but we had three or four forwards in there who didn't understand the concept of that. They were going into contact and placing the ball, but we had three players out of the seven who didn't know how to ruck and didn't have a clue what they were doing on that side of things.

In our first match against Saracens, I did manage to create one try with a 50-yard break but we just couldn't get hold of the ball and you can't keep defending all the time against a good side like Saracens. We scored two tries but both of them came out of nothing – it was just instinct. But for the rest of the game we chased shadows. We lost that match 26–14 and moved into the Plate competition.

The tournament certainly left me blowing a bit. It was a bit of a rude awakening for me, especially in the rucks and mauls, but the experience didn't put me off a move to Cardiff some 12 months later. Bradford went to the sevens two years later and won it. I spoke to some of the players who told me, 'We never went into contact. Before it got near to that we threw it over our heads, anywhere so we didn't go into contact.'

After the terrible start to our Super League campaign and our defeat in the Challenge Cup final we then won 13 games on the trot but it was really papering over the cracks. The players knew something wasn't right.

I suppose that 2000 season was summed up by a game at the start of September when St Helens came to Headingley and beat us 35–20. That loss to St Helens, after we led 20–12, was our first home defeat since May and although we won a few games to go into the play-offs, we were never very confident and failed to make the Grand Final.

Saints were reigning champions at the time and we were undone by three tries, two of them from Paul Newlove, in a devastating six-minute spell in the final quarter which turned the game on its head.

Following that, we won just one of our four remaining games in that campaign, which included a 18–6 defeat by the London Broncos in the final game of the regular season.

However, we still managed to finish fourth in the table and qualify for the play-offs. We had picked up a couple of injuries and although we managed to beat Castleford in the first play-off game, 22–14, it was a different story in the next match against the Bradford Bulls. By half-time we trailed 20–6 and eventually lost 46–12, which ended our season.

The club was pretty much in turmoil at the time. In the week of the game, Dean Lance was accused by Paul Sterling at an industrial tribunal of racial discrimination for not selecting him in the first-team squad. He was eventually found guilty of 'unconscious racism' and the club found guilty of not investigating Sterling's claims properly. In December, Leeds were ordered to pay compensation and reinstate him but he didn't play for them again. You could feel the club falling apart.

It was a disappointing time for me and other members of the team. The way we failed in 2000 made me believe that perhaps we were not, in the short term anyway, going to make that leap to become Grand Final winners and it encouraged me to start to look harder for a new career in union.

Every two or three seasons you get a lull at clubs as players retire or move on but that wasn't the case at Leeds. They weren't rebuilding – for me it was a case of, 'This place isn't right.' Towards the end, I'd lost a little bit of enjoyment. I was frustrated with what was happening because I felt passionate about the club. I felt the Leeds Rhinos could be so much more and I lost confidence in what the club were trying to achieve. I didn't see it could be put right over the next couple of years and that was the main reason I decided to leave. The lure of rugby union was becoming stronger.

I had always planned to go to union, and it would be wrong to give the impression that the disillusionment I felt at Leeds was instrumental in my decision: it wasn't.

Many people thought I, and others, could play league in the summer and union in the winter and although I contemplated that for a while, the idea never really got off the ground. You only need to look at the workload that the union boys have had in the last few years to realise it was impossible. In England the players are campaigning for a ten-week off-season. Just ten weeks! Hardly enough time to develop a rugby league career.

I think the idea of playing in Wales and for the Welsh national team was the biggest draw to me rather than the sport of rugby union. Having the opportunity to represent my country and to run out at the magnificent Millennium Stadium when it was full were the keys to my decision to actively, rather than passively, pursue a career in rugby union.

Things had changed so much since the game of union went professional in 1995 and I knew that although switching codes had been no more than a dream while I was growing up, I could now make it a reality. I suppose it was always in my mind, even before I played in the 1995 rugby league World Cup when we were based in Cardiff for much of the tournament. I don't want to give the impression that playing for Wales at rugby league didn't mean an awful lot: it did. When Clive Griffiths made me captain of the Wales team there was no prouder person. To play for Wales at any sport would have meant a lot to me.

In that 2000 tournament we went training at the Millennium Stadium before the New Zealand game and the rugby union lads were training there as well. I met Rob Howley, Neil Jenkins and Martyn Williams and I had a photoshoot with Jenks. I liked them and really got on well with them. When you only see players like that on the television you have reservations about how you will take to them but when I met them they were just normal guys. Neil was great and Rob was a gentleman. That was just before we played as a league team in front of 17,000 and I remember looking around that stadium and knowing that someday I wanted to come back with guys like Rob Howley and play in it when it was full. It made me realise that I would have to make my mind up very soon. I also knew deep down that playing for Wales at rugby league I would never have the opportunity of playing at the Millennium Stadium in front of 70,000 people with a nation of many more millions behind me. Deep inside me, I needed that opportunity. I needed the chance to test myself at the highest level in rugby union. I also liked the game, it was appealing to me, so I was in no doubt it was something I wanted to do.

The move to union wasn't the first time I had thought about turning my back on rugby league in England, although the time before, I turned down a new life for myself in Australia. The prospect of moving to Australia came up when my career was at a crossroads, following the 2000 Rugby League World Cup. A great friend of mine, Adrian Morley, had recently made the move Down Under and when the idea of signing a contract with union came closer to reality there were further offers from Australia to consider.

Adrian had a tough time in his first year and I didn't think it was fair to take Becky away from her friends and family. I don't think she was over-keen and to be honest neither was I. Ultimately, I realised it wasn't something which I had a burning desire to do, so it was better not to go if the conditions were less than perfect. The burning desire in my heart was to play for Wales.

Dean Lance parted company with the club in April 2001, not long after the start of the new season, and Daryl Powell took over. I had about three or four games under him, got injured and then left. I got on great with Daryl but too much had happened at the club that I didn't feel was right. I had a lot of respect for him and even though I was adamant I wanted to go to rugby union, I think if we'd sat down and had a heart to heart, I might have stayed.

At the time, I had a pretty good relationship with the people at Leeds like Gary Hetherington, Paul Caddick, the owner, and marketing executive David Howes.

Everyone knew of my desire to, one day, leave league and play union. I had spoken to them about it before so when I came to talk to them it wasn't a bolt out of the blue. I started the process by having a chat to Gary and explaining what I wanted to do. I told him that I wanted to play for Wales at the Millennium Stadium and represent them at the Rugby World Cup. I explained that I didn't want to do it in a half-hearted way. I wanted to have a real dig at it, to give it a real go and if I could do it straightaway so much the better.

Leeds were in turmoil at the time and I could see it would take time to turn things around. In fact, I think it took them four years to recover from the problems.

I was in my mid-20s and I believed the time was right to go. There was a Rugby World Cup two years down the line and I knew if I wanted to play in that tournament, I couldn't leave it much longer.

I do regret not having one last game at Leeds, to say goodbye to the fans, but injury got in the way of that. I had been through so much with those fans, including our incredible trip to Wembley two years earlier. However, I sustained a wrist injury in a match against Huddersfield about eight or nine games into the season and I was out for three months, the longest I had ever been on the sidelines. There's no doubt that the injury increased the pace of the move.

Tom Carroll was my agent at the time, so I rang Tom up and said, 'I've made my mind up.' I wanted to switch and asked him to see what was out there.

As the speculation had been raging about my move for a few years I was pretty confident the WRU would be interested in a deal, especially as the 2003 World Cup was starting to appear on the horizon. Unlike any other player to move before me, and with the same sort of deal that saw Andy Farrell move to union in 2005, things were always going to be a little more complicated. I couldn't just find a club and do the deal. My move to Wales was always going to be in the hands of the Welsh Rugby Union and it was up to them to find me a club where I could be based. Essentially I knew I was going to be employed by both the WRU and a new club, which made me unique in the Welsh game at the time.

The contract was similar to the ones they have in the southern hemisphere with their union players. It didn't really affect me on a day-to-day basis but it always meant that I was an employee of the Welsh Rugby Union rather than the club (Cardiff as it turned out) I played for. I know in the past there were stories about me joining Saracens in England or even Llanelli in Wales but when it came to the move most of the negotiations were carried out with the WRU. The transfer fee was clearly quite significant and as the WRU were paying the majority of the transfer fee, they were the ones who would make the most headway.

Glanmor Griffiths, who was chairman of the WRU, was leading the negotiations and they were saying they wanted me to play at Cardiff. I couldn't really argue with that, even if I wanted to. Clearly Cardiff are a massive side so why would I be unhappy to sign for them? I didn't have a tie to Llanelli or Swansea anyway so I was more than happy that the WRU were recommending Cardiff to me. I didn't know too much about the way the club game worked in Wales, so I was going into that side of it blindfolded. My attitude was to suck it and see.

I don't regret leaving the move until 2001 and I am always a person who backs his decisions. I had a memorable time in rugby league, but my priority was then to prove myself in union and that meant breaking into the Cardiff side. My first big meeting was with Glanmor and the Cardiff owner, Peter Thomas, who were very keen to make it happen. The salary the WRU were offering wasn't the biggest consideration. Obviously I didn't want to take a pay cut at that stage in my career, who would? But I didn't make the move to make my fortune.

Every move I have made has been lateral in terms of salary and the move to Wales was no different. I know some people believe I took millions but it wasn't the case. I didn't go any higher than my salary at Leeds or any lower. The transfer fee was big but I didn't set it. In the end it was around £750,000, which was a fortune in rugby terms, especially for a player who hadn't played the game before! It hasn't been matched since and I don't think that figure will be reached again. It was silly money but then there wasn't any way around it.

Another huge backer of the move was Wales coach Graham Henry. I don't think it could have happened without his support. Graham was adamant he wanted me in the Wales team. He'd seen quite a few games I had played in league and even more tapes. It was certainly strange to be carrying out many of the negotiations with a national coach, rather than a club one. I suppose Andy Farrell was in the same position in 2005 when he moved from Wigan to the RFU and Saracens. Graham was talking about Wales this and Wales that but I was thinking, 'I haven't even played one minute of union yet!'

He was talking about Wales before Cardiff and that was very difficult for me. I know Andy Farrell was keen to stress that he was never thinking he would walk straight into the England team as he'd done nothing in union and it was the same for me back in 2001. In many ways I would have been much more comfortable negotiating with Cardiff and then coming in and playing six months of club rugby before even thinking about the international game. I still think that would have been the best way and definitely the right way of starting a new career in a new sport. That's what Jason Robinson did. I wasn't that interested in Wales at the time as all I wanted to do was learn the game.

In July when Great Britain and England coach David Waite called a training squad for that autumn's series against Australia, I knew I could only join up with that squad if I was going to be available for the series in October. That decision to rule myself out of the Ashes series was compounded by the fact that I also had a wrist operation in July, my arm being in plaster for six weeks, ensuring I would miss Leeds' remaining Super League matches.

I met David and he said he really wanted me to play for Great Britain in the autumn of 2001 when the Australians were due to arrive. He understood that I was on the verge of a move to union but he asked me to play in the Australia series and go after that. But I told him that if I was to go, it would have to be as soon as possible. The World Cup was in 2003 and I wanted to have at least 18 months under my belt before the squad was announced. So to stay with league until after the Australia series would, I felt, delay my move for too long. Regrettably, I had to tell David I wouldn't be available and that was the first time the public knew for certain I would be playing my next game of rugby in union, rather than league.

David was very good. He said he understood exactly why I was making the move. I assured him it was nothing to do with money so there wasn't anything he or anyone else could do to persuade me otherwise. It was a rugby decision I had to make.

I suppose David was one of the only people in league who tried to talk me out of it. He had nothing to gain financially, while Leeds did, and like any national coach he was trying to get me to play for Great Britain. But once I had given my reasons for going, he accepted it. He wished me all the best, thanked me for coming to see him and I thanked him for the way he was: a complete gentleman.

After the negotiations were completed, Graham Henry spoke about me in his column in *The Mirror*. Graham said:

Iestyn Harris created Welsh rugby union history by becoming the first high-profile, born-and-bred rugby league player to switch to the 15-man game in Wales.

I'm still getting to know him, but from what I've seen he is mature, modest and very appreciative of those who've helped him down the years.

He's looking forward to a new challenge by trying to emulate his huge achievements in league in the union game. But as Iestyn said himself that won't be easy. He talked about Jonathan Davies, a mate of his with whom he played rugby league early in his career.

Jonathan was a world class union player but when he switched codes everyone was writing him off. It took him 18 months to adjust to league but he became a magnificent, influential player. Jonathan's example will let Iestyn know it is possible to switch codes successfully.

Iestyn has lots of experience as captain of Leeds and Wales and I'm confident he'll handle the switch because he knows it will take hard work and time.

I'm sure I can speak for the Welsh squad, management and players, and say we're delighted at Iestyn's decision. We're all excited about the opportunity of working with him.

The WRU and chairman Glanmor Griffith have shown in signing Iestyn they are committed to making the national team a success. Iestyn will help us compete with the world's best and we're thrilled he will be helping to better our national game.

But the move didn't go down well in every part of Welsh rugby and to the east, in Newport, their owner Tony Brown explained that he was against my move. Tony said, 'It was only three years ago that Cardiff and Swansea walked away from the WRU. I find it incredible that the Union has been prepared to reward them in this way. Nobody in the WRU ever came up to us and asked if we were interested in signing Iestyn Harris for £100,000 a year.

'It is unfair on the clubs who remained loyal to the WRU at a difficult time. We brought players like Shane Howarth and Peter Rogers back to Wales at our own expense. It seems that the WRU does not like those clubs who are showing a degree of independence.

'This is something we should be looking at as a group of clubs. Money is meant to be tight, but Cardiff are getting £400,000 a year more from the WRU than any other side and it is unnecessarily divisive.'

Glanmor Griffiths replied on my behalf, saying, 'Nobody is getting special treatment. We have funds available should any other club identify a player they are interested in signing and who also attracts the interest of Wales coach Graham Henry.

'When Iestyn signed we made history. This is a red letter day for our game, the boot is on the other foot now. We lost two or three of our top players to league every year and it was difficult to overcome at times.'

I even 'went south' with the full backing of the Leeds Rhinos. Chief executive Gary Hetherington said, 'Naturally we are disappointed to be losing Iestyn. He has been a terrific servant to the club, but we fully understand his desire to continue his career with the Welsh Rugby Union and Cardiff. We have tried to negotiate a deal which will reflect his standing and ability in the game.'

All that was then left was for me to provide my dad's birth certificate, which showed he was born in Pontywaun, near Cross Keys. A few years earlier the Welsh Rugby Union had been embroiled in the 'Grannygate' affair when it was discovered that a couple of players, including Shane Howarth, had played for Wales when they weren't eligible.

Once I had signed, the publicity was incredible. Every newspaper, every radio station and every television channel seemed to be talking about my arrival and I hadn't even made one pass, run or kick in rugby union. I remember thinking that whatever I do in my first few games will be exaggerated one way or another and so it proved. But I also knew there was nothing I could do about it.

Initially I met Graham Henry a couple of times as I wanted to be absolutely sure we were on the same wavelength about the game. It was crucial the national coach understood my thoughts on how long it would take for me to learn the game.

Graham said he felt it was really important I came straightaway, in 2001, two years before the World Cup. He said that he believed it would take me at least 12 to 18 months to adapt to the game, as I had never played it before. I was really happy with that analysis and he told me he was not going to rush things. Unfortunately it didn't quite work out that way when I put pen to paper.

SIX

MY DAYS AT THE ARMS PARK

The coach at Cardiff was Rudy Joubert but he wasn't involved in any of the negotiations and I only got to meet him once I had signed. When I did meet him I found him very matter-of-fact. He was very scientific about the game. He saw one way to play and that was it. He didn't seem to really care about the players and I think he was a little bit reluctant to take me. His attitude was, 'I don't want someone who's never played the game before, I'm not interested in him.'

Geraint John was his assistant and I got on reasonably well with him. But at the time they were in conflict. Joubert's attitude was, 'I'm head coach and you are assistant coach. I don't want you involved at all, I'm my own man.'

So Geraint John was against Joubert and wanted him to fail because he knew that, at the end of the year, if Cardiff were doing well and Rudy Joubert carried on, he would be out of a job. Geraint's attitude was, 'I'm not getting involved in this, it's nothing to do with me.' There was a lot of sniping and I was just wondering what was going on. I was getting very little to no help at all.

I did a little bit of work with Jonathan Davies. He went through

125

a few videos with me but only a small amount. I got a bit of help from Clive Griffiths but Clive had his work to do with Wales and as I was with Cardiff most of the time it was difficult for him.

There was talk in the press about a kicking coach coming in, a specialist to teach me about the rucks and mauls and specialists coming in to help me with this and that. It was all talk, nothing ever happened. I was pushed into Cardiff and the view seemed to be, 'Oh, Cardiff will deal with it.'

Graham Henry was chatting to me about how he wanted Wales to play but really it's all about learning to do it on the training field and I never got that opportunity. It was a 'suck it and see' approach. When things were going right, great, but when things were going wrong, nobody was explaining to me why it was wrong. It took me a year to work it out on my own.

Also, the position I would play hadn't been resolved. Jonathan Davies was certainly hoping I wouldn't be put under pressure and handed the number 10 shirt. He said, 'We don't even know what position he will slot into. I imagine that inside-centre will suit him best, but it will take a while to find out. There's talk of him making his Welsh debut against Tonga in November. I don't know how much club rugby he will have played by then but you may as well draw a target on his chest for the Tongans to aim at.' Little did he, or I, know that the Tonga game would be my second Test, and my second at outside-half!

I had had an operation on my wrist so I arrived in Wales with a plaster on my arm. Like Andy Farrell four years later, I arrived in union with an injury and couldn't play for the first few weeks. That ensured I had a five-week build-up to my first game for Cardiff, which made it even worse, as the expectation seemed to grow and grow.

Jonathan Davies, my teammate with Warrington and Wales (league) realised how tough it would be for me. Writing in the *Independent on Sunday* he said:

In a way, Iestyn Harris ought to be grateful that his arm

injury will keep him out of action until October. The season that has started this weekend is bewildering enough to someone who has spent his entire career in rugby union, let alone one about to play it for the first time in his life.

I have no doubt that Iestyn will be a success with Cardiff and Wales. I've watched his career closely since he was a youngster at Warrington when I played there and I have long considered him to be one of the great rugby talents of his generation. We're great friends, so I may be a little biased, but I'm looking forward to helping him adjust to his new career.

Being able to just look and learn from the sideline will be of great benefit to him as he absorbs the different rules, attitudes and tactics, particularly as the mess in which the season starts in Wales ought to have become clearer by the time he is ready to join the fray.

Union will be as difficult for Iestyn to get accustomed to as league was for me 12 years ago, but I had two distinct advantages. I joined the best team in league at the time. They were quite brilliant, and I could slowly fit into a set-up good enough to put up with my learning difficulties. Cardiff have some great players but have been underachieving and, with a new coach in the South African Rudy Joubert, will take some time to find their feet.

Iestyn might find he is under immediate pressure to make a contribution to a team not quite sure of themselves. Everyone agrees he will need time to adjust but I doubt if he will get it.

I was a target for all the hard men when I went to league and had to take the knocks, but I had the protection and know-how of the top team to back me up. Iestyn won't have that. His skill as a footballer won't stop him being exposed that early in his learning process.

The other advantage I had was that the league

programme is simple and straightforward. It is far more competitively intense than the club season in union, and you know that there is no such thing as an easy game.

In union there are so many different competitions going on that matches differ in importance from week to week, and with the top players switching from club to country duties as well it can be very confusing.

To introduce the Celtic League and start the season in the middle of August is ridiculous. The fans are not ready for it and neither, I suspect, are the players.

When I actually came to make my debut it was a couple of weeks before the 2001 Autumn internationals and I didn't want to be involved in those Test matches.

My family was also an important factor in my move to Wales. I don't think I needed to ask the opinion of my parents, sister or granddad. I knew they would be behind me every step of the way, whether I had chosen to stay in league or move to union but I'm also pretty sure they were delighted with my decision. And in any story of my life I would never want to forget the role that Becky played.

I was lucky enough to meet Becky during the darkest time for me when I was training at four in the morning, having been put out in the cold by Warrington in 1996. I met her on a Sunday night at a bar in Oldham and we hit it off straight away. She didn't know much about rugby league and didn't know who I was, although I think some of her friends did. We just started chatting, I gave her a lift home and her dad ended up kicking me out of the house! In a nice way – what would you do with a rugby player in your house? I was in the kitchen having a coffee and he came in and said, 'Right, I'm off to bed now, so if you wouldn't mind leaving!' Her family aren't interested in sport, which was quite good because you don't want to walk into a house where the father starts talking about rugby. It was quite refreshing: I was 19 and just someone who was dating their daughter.

I was at a low point and she was brilliant and helped me through that six months. Our relationship became quite strong. I was living with my parents at the time and after that with some friends. I can't say we had the tidiest house in the world so when Becky turned up she'd spend most of the time cleaning!

We had a good time together. It was the right thing for me at the time for us to have our own lives as well as seeing each other – I was still relatively young, as was she.

She came down for the cup final in 1999 and I suppose I was lucky that she had a good circle of friends at Leeds and was big friends with Barrie McDermott's wife, Jenny. We didn't move in together until 2001 and in June, Catrin, our daughter, came along, changing my outlook on life dramatically.

In many ways we had a tough time because Catrin was only three months old when we moved to Wales in September 2001. This meant the pressure was on Becky but she responded amazingly well, doing everything she could to make the move a success. Both sets of parents were living up north and I was away with Wales so it made it tough for her but she knew I wanted to move and supported me all the way. The timing, in purely sporting terms, was perfect for me but it could have come at a better time for her. It was a huge decision for us both. I did have family in Wales but I wouldn't class them as immediate family. We moved there and didn't have a lot of people around us but we made that decision together.

We moved to Cardiff with trepidation, Becky was worried about the move, as was I. We didn't know anyone there and we didn't even know which areas of the city we should look in for a new house. In the end, with the help of Jonathan Davies and his then fiancée Helen, we managed to buy in the right area, finding a wonderful house with some wonderful friends nearby.

Jonathan and Helen showed us around and Becky became good friends with Helen, which was a big factor in settling in so quickly.

We found a house within a month, although it felt as if we were caught in a bit of a whirlwind as I was trying to learn a new game in amongst the big move.

My first game of union came on 20 October 2001 when I was a half-time substitute in Cardiff's 28–25 defeat at Llanelli, ironically a comeback game for one of my former Wales rugby league teammates, Scott Quinnell, who had been on the injured list since the Lions tour the summer before.

When I returned to the dressing-room at Cardiff Arms Park after we had beaten Glasgow on my full debut for Cardiff in the Heineken Cup I was on top of the world. Well, who wouldn't be? I had kicked off a new sport by scoring 31 points which included a hat-trick of tries as my new team romped home 46–7.

In the newspapers the next day, the journalists were talking about 'the new miracle man' turning in a performance 'to pave the way for a first Wales cap against Argentina in two weeks' and I was starting to believe that my move to rugby union could in fact have a fairy-tale start. But, of course, this talk was ridiculous, it was just one game. However, the reaction was perhaps typical of the passion and feelings of a Welsh nation that had been starved of a Grand Slam since 1978.

Seven days earlier, I had been on the bench for the game against Llanelli and kicked a penalty two minutes after coming on but the Glasgow match was the first time I'd started a game. I was joined in the team that day by my old rugby league mate Anthony Sullivan who also ran in a hat-trick. Anthony had played for Cardiff before in an off-season but this was his debut as a full-time player as well.

It was a very free-flowing game, much closer to the sort of rugby I had played in league rather than the union style I was to settle into. In that first game against Glasgow, I was still playing off rugby league instincts. There was a lot of space – everything went well and I scored three decent tries. From then it was just a whirlwind. I was whisked off immediately to a press conference and it seemed over the next few days that every newspaper and radio station was talking about me. I certainly wasn't ready to be thrust into the spotlight that way and so quickly but I suppose the publicity I got explains in a small way how much the Welsh public love rugby union.

It was really difficult for me, to say, 'Hold on, I have so much to learn, I have achieved nothing.'

In the summer of 2005, Andrew Farrell was trying to get that message across to the RFU and England's fans. I know exactly what he meant. In reality that incredible start was the worst thing that could have happened to me. It would have been much easier to have had a few lower profile performances, a couple of steady matches to ease my way into union.

My intention was to hold my own for five, six or seven games and start to get a feel for the way the game should be played. I was still throwing out long balls, like the ones I had thrown out in league, and I had no understanding of the tackle area. Against Glasgow those long passes were coming off, we were scoring tries and creating space. But, as everyone in union knows, you can have free-flowing open games and you can have far more technical games in which you can't do that. At the time, I didn't realise that.

In England, Jason Robinson had made the same move as me but he was lucky to be introduced into the England team the easy way. A substitute performance against Italy was followed by two others against Scotland and France, while for me one game of union for Cardiff had the Welsh public and the media excited like never before. In fact, Jason started for the British and Irish Lions before he made his full England debut in the autumn internationals of 2001, eight months after first joining the England squad.

Of course it would be wrong to blame Cardiff for the way things worked out for me. They had paid a big transfer fee and they needed me to deliver. The grand old club had seen better times and before I arrived they were not doing well in Europe, having already lost to Montferrand and been thumped by Munster in the Celtic League.

The Cardiff honeymoon lasted just seven days but it was pretty clear that either the Welsh public hadn't seen or didn't want to know about the return leg with Glasgow, where we lost 47–32. After my incredible day a week earlier, it was the Glasgow outside-half, Tommy Hayes, who took centre stage, scoring 32 points in a defeat that knocked us out of Europe. Graham Henry went to that return leg and even though we did lose, it was another free-flowing game and I managed to score another try. It was still very similar to a league game.

Even though we lost, I didn't feel out of my depth. At the time I didn't really know what I was doing in rucks and mauls and got caught a few times. When I went into contact I didn't understand the principles of recycling the ball. In fact, in those first few games, I used to just throw the ball back. I didn't know about ball placement or which side to get your body on, things like that.

We needed victory in Glasgow to maintain a realistic chance of qualification for the quarter-finals and the defeat meant our fate was out of our own hands. Our only hope was that Montferrand would fail to snatch another point.

Even the run-up to those first two games was difficult. Having arrived with a wrist injury, I just did five or six weeks of work with the Cardiff fitness coach Huw Wiltshire. Trying to learn the game just through a fitness regime was not ideal. I only had a fitness test on my wrist on the Tuesday leading into the game against Llanelli. When I played that first game I'd only had three sessions with a ball and, looking back, it was the wrong thing for the team.

Luckily for me, Cardiff had a very simple style of play. The coach, Rudy Joubert, didn't believe in having a lot of different moves. We had two set calls and that was it. At the time that seemed fine but looking back I am flabbergasted that Cardiff did so well with a play book that only contained two moves! It was easier for me, but I was still playing the way I had always played in rugby league.

I have a lot of people to thank for the way I survived those opening few months in union, not least my half-back partner at

Cardiff and Wales, Rob Howley. Rob was really good. He took a lot of pressure off me that year with his box kicking and the way we worked together, which probably younger scrum-halfs wouldn't have been able to do. At times when there was a lot of pressure on me, I turned to him. But although he was a world-class player, there was only so much he could do.

The rest of the players at Cardiff were fantastic. Despite that big transfer fee, the Cardiff boys couldn't have done any more and none of them held it against me. Obviously opponents wanted to knock my head off and you expect that. But the teammates in any side I was involved with in union were as good as gold.

When I arrived at the club I was vying for the outside-half spot with Nicky Robinson. He is a great kid and was fine with me – we used to do a lot of work together. Rudy Joubert was critical of his outside halves in that year. He was very structured and he didn't want any variation. From scrums all he wanted us to do was catch and pass, he didn't want us to run. During that time, Nicky and I worked well.

I found the training a little bit strange. In league we'd maybe train for 45 minutes or an hour but at a high intensity, whereas Rudy Joubert went for long, often mundane, sessions. They didn't do the high-intensity stuff I had done in league and I found that very hard to get used to. In league you might only be out on the training field for an hour but for the whole of that hour it would be 'go go go'. At Cardiff you might be out there for two or two and a half hours and it would be stop-start. Things did change and at the end of my union career the sessions were of a very high intensity, exactly as league is and was.

Back in 2001, union hadn't been full-time for too long, especially in Wales, and they felt full-time meant being out on the training field for two or two and a half hours a day. Going into that was difficult for me. I remember Anthony Sullivan and I used to chat about the training sessions and get frustrated with their length and lack of intensity. The skills we used to do in league we were not doing in union.

There was also too much contact. Sometimes we might have two or three contact sessions in a week and that was tough to get used to. I wasn't used to that level of contact in league training sessions and I'm not sure that knocking the stuffing out of your teammates all week was the best way to prepare for a big game.

There are some physical players in union, so it was hard enough taking that much contact on a weekend without taking it again in training. I do agree you need some sort of contact but I think it must be controlled rather than an out-and-out bashing of each other for 40 minutes at a time.

At Cardiff we used to always play against the Under-21s in a full-on match in midweek. It was that, as much as the games, which was difficult to get used to. In league we used to have the initial 40 or 45 minutes of really intense training and then you'd do your own work outside of that, whether it was going to the gym, agility work or kicking. At Cardiff, I was doing these two and a half hour sessions and then trying to work on my kicking. I used to have to put in a lot of time on restarts with backs coach Geraint John as this was something I'd never done before in my life. More and more they became an important part of the game. If you haven't done restarts before it is a very difficult skill to master. I must have spent an hour and a half a day on it, time I could have been using on other things.

Even the way I goalkicked had completely changed, so I couldn't even fall back on that as a skill I could bring from league. The changes that were made to my goalkicking in union were for the better as it is a far more technical skill in the 15-man game. Things were more advanced in union. Goalkicking was obviously very important in league but it is crucial in union, so the coaches ensured far more time was spent on it. In league it was pretty much, 'You are the goalkicker, get on with it, practise yourself', but in union it was cross-sectioned and every kick analysed.

At the very start of my time in union I was tinkering with my kicking style and it took some time for me to recover. When you tinker with your goalkicking you need to go backwards before you go forwards. In those early games I was missing kicks I should have got. That tinkering made life difficult for me in the short term. Nicky Robinson was going through the same process before we started getting to grips with it.

In my early days at Cardiff, I was lucky that one of the greatest goalkickers in either code, Neil Jenkins, was around. He was doing a little bit of the goalkicking coaching at Cardiff at the time because he was injured – in fact, he was out for the full year.

He helped out a little bit as did Geraint John and Clive Griffiths, who was still involved with me. I did take the goalkicking extremely seriously. Despite my good record with the boot in league, I knew I had a lot to learn, so I was keen to take on board any advice they could give me. No matter how good you feel you are at something, you can always get better, although there wasn't much cooperation between Cardiff and the Wales team at that time as the club versus country row was raging.

Following the autumn internationals in 2001, I returned to action with Cardiff in something of a daze but it was time to get stuck into the routine of club rugby. This was where I was going to get the experience to work through the problems I had encountered in those early matches for Wales.

In that first season it was difficult to leave Cardiff for a few games with Wales and then to return to the club again. I think the structure of rugby union within the home nations makes things unnecessarily tough on the players as you might have three or four peaks in a season rather than building to one big climax. This was one of the reasons I found it tough in club rugby. You'd have two or three big games and then they would rest everyone for the easier ones so it was difficult to get into a rhythm. Many of the international players were thinking about Test matches when they were playing for their clubs. You needed to be in there quite a while to understand it.

My first game back with Cardiff was a 16–12 win over Neath and a few successful kicks went over from my boot. A draw with Bridgend began a great run around the Christmas period. We were adrift, but tries from Rhys Williams and Jamie Robinson hauled us back into the game and my conversion gave us a share of the spoils. We beat Pontypridd before pulling off the best win of my first season in rugby union, a 26–20 win over Montferrand in the Heineken Cup. It was a performance that showed what we were capable of in Europe.

That victory was something else. It was a magnificent day, particularly for Rhys Williams, who had been blamed in some quarters for our earlier loss to them in France. I always thought Rhys was a sensational player and he scored two tries against Montferrand that day. He brought a flash of inspiration to the game when he collected from Rob Howley on halfway, kicked ahead and won the race for the line.

I really haven't got a bad word to say about Rhys. He was certainly one of the players I felt could do just as well in league. He would be in any team I would pick and was a good guy to have alongside you. That try against Montferrand demonstrated why he was such a dangerous attacker. When you are playing in the big games you need players who can do something special and that's where Rhys comes in. He always had that extra yard of space. When you've got those older players around you also need guys like Rhys. He was a key member of the Wales Grand Slam side in 2005 and were it not for injury he would have taken his place in the last triumphant game against Ireland at the Millennium Stadium.

Unfortunately, not even that magnificent win against Montferrand could keep Cardiff in Europe that season. We could still have sneaked into the quarter-finals by winning our final game at Northampton but it wasn't to be. I remember Rob Howley made one scintillating break midway through the first half but I lost my footing and couldn't get on the end of his run. Both myself and Anthony Sullivan went close in the second half and even when Northampton went down to 14 men, after Andrew Blowers had received a yellow card, we couldn't force the advantage home.

To get through we not only had to win but score three tries. If we hadn't needed those three tries I'm sure we would have won the game as we passed up a number of penalty chances. I was kicking everything that day but when the penalty chances came along we ran everything. Normally we would have ground out a victory with those chances but it would have been no good to us. That's sometimes how the Heineken Cup goes. Although we were playing good rugby it wasn't enough; it was unfortunate that we needed those tries. We lost 26–15, all our points coming from my right boot, and that defeat finally signalled the end of our participation in the Heineken Cup.

I thought we were really unlucky not to qualify for the knockout stages that season as I believed we had a very good team. Guys like Rob Howley, David Young and Jonathan Humphreys were good, seasoned professionals. Even Neil Jenkins, although he wasn't playing for Cardiff that year, was still very influential and had an input. Neil was part of a large group of players who had been there and done it. I arrived at a club with a good team and it was excellent to play with them.

I know Rob had his grievances with Rudy Joubert and there were other players who had their views on the way the side should be playing. I think Rob made the decision to go to Wasps as he knew he didn't have too long left in the game and he wanted to win trophies. He felt he needed a move to do this, saying, 'I'm going to Wasps to win medals, to win the Premiership and to show Wasps rugby club the commitment they have shown to me.' He got that success by winning the Zurich title and the Heineken Cup with them, so it was the perfect move for him.

I knew Rob was thinking about moving as he was getting frustrated with the way the game was played at Cardiff. We were going into games naively, thinking we could play this open style when a lot of the time it depended on how the referee controlled the game. It was very difficult. Rudy felt we should just play what we saw in front of us but sometimes you need a structure. We'd lose the ball so often in the second and third phases because we didn't have that structure. That let us down in the end but we did have a very, very good side that year. I was really pleased coming into a Cardiff team that had such a good base. I thought the side could develop and go on to the next level but then so many of the good players left at the end of the season.

Before they left, there was a Welsh Cup final to try and win. I had enjoyed my dream of playing at the Millennium Stadium for Wales back in November but I also took great pleasure from the experience with Cardiff in my first season. Unfortunately, as with Wales in November, it was something of a painful experience. We played local rivals and holders Newport in the quarter-final. I turned in an indifferent performance with the boot, missing four from eight, so I was grateful for a late try from my friend Rob Howley. Four minutes from time he sprinted over from 20 metres, catching the Newport defence napping, to book Cardiff's place in the last four with a 20–14 win.

It was the very short journey from the Arms Park to the Millennium Stadium for the semi against Pontypridd. The semi-finals were back-to-back on that day and I will look back on that game against Pontypridd as one we should have won. We'd scored two really good tries in the first half and went into the dressing-room on top. We just said, 'It's ours, we just have to take it.' But we came out in the second half and they kicked us to death. They pinned us right back in the corners and we were getting frustrated. Brett Davey kicked everything in sight, notching up 25 points to send them through.

I don't know what it was. In the first half we were by far the better team and we just couldn't take it on in the second half. Perhaps we were just a little too confident at half-time. I suppose our disappointment was compounded by the fact that we had beaten them in the league and at Sardis Road a month earlier, 21–18, to complete a double over them. On that day, I managed to create a try for Anthony Sullivan but when it came to the Millennium Stadium semi-final we couldn't repeat the trick. They were the outsiders but they had players in their team, like Brent

Cockbain and Mefin Davies, who were to feature in Wales's Grand Slam success in 2005.

With the cup gone we ended up winning just four of our last seven games so by the time we arrived at the last day of the season all we could do by beating Llanelli was hand the title to Newport. In the end, we couldn't even do that. We took an early lead but they pinned us back and took the title by beating us 28–25. Llanelli had more to gain from winning the game than we did and that may have been the crucial factor. Every game we lost that year, I can look back and say we should have won, so there was no real reason why Cardiff couldn't have been champions that season.

At the end of this first season I still didn't fully understand the role of outside-half. I didn't know the real principles behind pinning the corners, when to kick and when not to. At times we could have kicked more and placed the ball in the corner because we had the pack to grind it out. But we hadn't got to grips with that. Under Rudy Joubert it was hard to play a new style. We had the team to go a long way in Europe and if Dai Young had been coaching that team rather than the one he inherited in the following season I think we would have gone a long way. It was frustrating.

I was left on the bench for that final win over Bridgend with Rob Howley coming on as substitute for Neil Jenkins as the former Wales legend started his first game for Cardiff for the first time since March a year earlier. Rudy said Jenks was back and he was going to give him a run. The season was over and I didn't see it as me being dropped as there was little to play for. It was about giving different players different games.

During the season there was unrelenting speculation about the future of Rudy and in the run-up to our 24–16 win over Aberavon in the Welsh Cup he went home to South Africa to be interviewed for the vacant post of Springboks coach. As it turned out, he left that summer after accepting an offer to return to his native South Africa and Dai Young took over.

I don't think Dai wanted to go in as head coach. He wanted to learn his trade and then become a head coach but your career rarely works out the way you plan it. He got offered the job and obviously took it but it was an incredibly difficult start for him. Dai didn't have any experience in coaching. But even as an inexperienced coach, if you have experienced players around you, you have half a chance. However, with so many experienced professionals now gone, it left him short of leaders. I knew Dai reasonably well and got on very well with him. He captained Wales in league when I played there and I always had and still do have a lot of respect for him.

Before we started the new campaign I went through a very strange pre-season. A groin injury I picked up against Neath robbed me of my chance to go on tour with Wales to South Africa in the summer. I had six weeks doing nothing to get over the injury, so I came back to Cardiff raring to go. But the relationship between Wales and their clubs was still difficult. It was bizarre. I had never been involved in a union pre-season before, and rather than it being with Cardiff, it ended up being with Wales.

Andy Hore had just come in as the Wales fitness coach and he arranged everything I did in that pre-season. Wales had picked a squad of 50, so you had the strange scenario of the internationals at Cardiff doing their pre-season in one part of the Arms Park and the rest of the Cardiff players in another. Can you imagine the situation? The Cardiff players would be working on their fitness on one side of the pitch and then the six or seven that were in the Wales squad were doing a fitness session Andy Hore had devised on the other side of the pitch. To this day, I will never understand it. The system created an unnecessary division at Cardiff and, I presume, at the other Welsh clubs.

I think pre-season is incredibly important in building team spirit, especially at Cardiff where we had lost so many of the big characters at our club. I wanted to train with my teammates and not just the ones who were in a 50-man Wales squad. The group at Cardiff had less chance to bond.

Because Andy Hore had lots of clubs and players to look after, we often had to take the sessions ourselves. He used to email either Rhys Williams or Martyn Williams, as they were the two who loved their computers, with the sessions, and they'd print it out and come to training. We'd do our ball work with Cardiff and then either Rhys or Martyn would read out what Andy Hore had sent through and just do it.

All of us talked about it and we were very uncomfortable with the system but we got on with it. We didn't speak to players at the other clubs but I presume they felt the same. Can you imagine a club where one group of players trains in one place under one regime and the rest train somewhere else? The guys at your club are the ones you go into battle with and you want to be training with them. They were doing one bit of hard work and we were doing another. Although we didn't create the situation, I think it caused a conflict and there were some in the Cardiff group who thought, 'Look at them, are they too good for us?' If the boot had been on the other foot it would have antagonised me as well. As it was, I was annoyed with the situation but there was nothing I could do about it.

What made it even more strange was that although the Wales players did their fitness work on their own they did their ball work with the rest of the Cardiff squad.

The structure simply didn't work. I don't think they do that now but I suppose it was symptomatic of the struggle rugby in Wales was having with professionalism. Andy Hore hadn't experienced what Welsh rugby was all about, neither had Steve Hansen or Scott Johnson, the other senior coach. I think the WRU were asking too much of the Welsh clubs.

We kicked off the 2002 season, my first full one with Cardiff, with a couple of home low-key friendly victories against Bourgogne and Bath but the real action in 2002 began in Connacht on 6 September when we suffered a heartbreaking 23–22 defeat. I was starting to find my feet but at the same time I was worried that so many of the club's senior players had left and about what it would mean for the team in that season. They were bringing in Under-21 players and asking them to step up to this level immediately. We didn't have as strong a squad and that was frustrating. Also in the background was the change in Welsh rugby in 2002–03. From almost the first game there was talk of the Cardiff rugby club I had joined becoming the Cardiff Blues, one of the new regional teams.

Initially the stories were about us merging with Pontypridd and it was frustrating for all the Cardiff players. We had a 24- or 25-man squad and you clearly don't need 50 players for one region. It was politics. I had a contract with Cardiff as everybody else did. Some of it was paid by Wales but it all came through Cardiff. Peter Thomas, the owner of the club, came in and sat all the players down and said, 'We don't know where we're going. We want to be the Cardiff Blues and merge with Pontypridd. The name will be changing and we're only going to want half the players, so some of you might lose your jobs but then again we might be staying as we are.' Some of the players were frightened to death. I'd only been there a year and all the members of the WRU committee who had been involved in my signing had gone, with David Moffatt coming in as chief executive.

The WRU were £50 million in debt and had to do something about it. The 150 people employed by the WRU were cut down to 60 within a week. They sold their grand offices in the middle of Cardiff and moved into a second-floor office in a back street to save money. They weren't paying bills left, right and centre. I remember sitting at home with my wife, saying, 'They could be cutting my contract.' They could have said, 'Let's push this £200,000 we're paying him aside and call it quits and let him go wherever he wants.' Becky and I were thinking, 'How are we going to pay our mortgage, the car, how are we going to eat?' It was so bad that at one point everyone was fearful of their livelihood. In the end, Pontypridd wouldn't merge and they stayed as they were but if they had, there were serious chances of things going wrong. It was a really difficult time.

On the field, we didn't have to wait too long for our first win. We beat the Borders 18–15 at Cardiff Arms Park. I played against Gregor Townsend and had the better of the day. I'd known Gregor for a few years. We were both sponsored by Reebok and had done a few photoshoots and events together so it was good to get to play against him.

He actually had a poor game that day. It was strange, as they scored two tries while I kicked six penalties to win the game. It was a good win for us as we had lost our first home game to Glasgow.

I was starting to understand the game a little more, to know when and why I needed to kick. It was coming together slowly and I remember the Borders game was very tactical. I had to rely on my kicking and it was the first time I'd managed to do that, so it was good to think I was getting there.

Richard Smith was my new half-back partner that season and he was going well until he was injured. Ryan Powell was going well as his replacement until he also picked up an injury. The team was OK when we were able to put out our strongest 15 but once we picked up injuries we started to struggle. Martyn Williams was back, which was a big positive, taking over the captaincy from Dai, who had retired from playing.

That season was the first time I got to play with Martyn and I soon realised what a great player he is. He is the sort of player who could have done very well in league as well. He's good with his hands, has good speed and he's one of those players who wants to be involved all the time. Martyn was a big help to me. He's not the type of player to give advice but if you need him, he'd be there. He is one of those players you enjoy playing with as he does the tough stuff not everyone is prepared to do. I was probably the least surprised person to see him named RBS Six Nations Player of the Tournament in 2005. Typical of Martyn, he refused to take the credit for himself and instead heaped the praise on the team when he received his award.

Despite our problems we had a good September with wins over

Leinster and Newport but that gave way to an awful October as we kicked off our Heineken Cup campaign with a 26–15 home defeat to Biarritz, who were one of the favourites for the tournament. We didn't play that badly; we were in the game for 60 or 70 minutes but they scored a try late on to take them away. Our only points came from five penalty goals.

The defeat to Biarritz was only Cardiff's second at home in 18 Heineken Cup matches stretching back to 1995. The step-up from Celtic League to Heineken Cup was just too much for some of the players. The side was simply too inexperienced to cope. Some had been fringe players for other clubs but came in and were first choice for Cardiff.

You get no second chances in the Heineken Cup. It looks like a competition with a pool stage and knockout but realistically it is knockout all the way, as one or two defeats can put you out. As soon as you lose at home you can just about forget it, so to go down to Biarritz at the Arms Park in the first game meant curtains for us.

I think the French are a different breed altogether. They are so athletic and sometimes they don't need to be as technically good as other sides. Teams like Cardiff and Wales need to be technically right to win. The French play with such flair, you think you've got them contained and they score two tries out of nothing. I am proud to say, though, that at no point in this Heineken Cup campaign, apart from Biarritz away, did we get thumped. We competed with them all but we were just a little bit under what we needed to be.

When you lose early on it can be a frustrating tournament. After that defeat by Biarritz we had to go to Ulster and win. Ulster are a very good side and Ravenhill is such a hard place to go and win.

Playing at Ulster on a Friday night is very tough, especially as we were in a must-win mentality after losing the first game. There was a lot of pressure on us but we were in the game for the majority of the 80 minutes. They just kept edging away and we kept getting more deflated as the game went on. The Irish provinces always recycle the ball exceptionally well and Ulster were no different. They just kept the ball and kept the pressure on. It turned out to be a really tough day. The spirit was still there and there was a fabulous commitment to defence but we eventually lost 25–6.

There we were thinking the Heineken Cup was over, yet we still had four games to go. What also didn't help us at that time was our tendency to pick up yellow and even red cards. Discipline was a major problem. Senior players were giving away too many penalties and at this level you just can't afford to drop down to 14 men. When we lost to Pontypridd 15–9, Peter Rogers' yellow card was the team's eighth sin-bin in nine competitive matches plus one sending-off. Dai Young spoke about it and in fact we all spoke about it, although it didn't change. By giving away penalties, we were constantly under the cosh. We were struggling anyway, so we couldn't cope with being one man down, especially in the pack, but it took a long time to improve.

The awful run ended in the Celtic League Cup quarter-final on 30 November after the autumn internationals when we beat Edinburgh 26–22. It was a team effort to savour as the club's spirit shone through the darkness of a 13-point deficit at the interval. Martyn Williams spearheaded a courageous second 40 minutes and from numbers 15 to 1 every member of the side contributed to an heroic effort that set up a Celtic League semi-final in Neath.

We went into the first game with that Edinburgh win behind us and in the knowledge that only a victory would keep us in the competition. A lack of strength in depth in the tight five placed too great an onus on the front-line troops that were available. Dai Young even had to come out of retirement to shore up the pack but we were going into the games with players who weren't up to the task. We were asking players to play above themselves and that is always a difficult situation.

Dai was frustrated. He had taken over as coach but didn't have the players to compete. In those circumstances it is hard to coach and realistically that year we would have been better off in the Parker Pen Cup, the second-tier European competition. As we came up against the top European teams, they had too much firepower for us. We always competed at home but when we played away we didn't have the experience or the team to do it.

You'd think our Heineken Cup campaign couldn't have got much worse but I think one of the most damaging weeks in the history of the great Cardiff club arrived in December when we lost at Northampton. With John Tait injured and Chris Stamatakis ill, there wasn't even second-row cover left for the replacements' bench at Franklin's Gardens. We had started well with two penalty goals but fell away, losing 25–11.

In the return match worse was to come as we were hammered 31–0. It was the first time in 30 years that any Cardiff senior team had failed to register points at the Arms Park. They just bulldozed us early on and we were missing tackles all over the park. The game was done and dusted after 20 minutes.

Forgetting about the Heineken Cup was all we could do but, returning to the Welsh Premiership, we lost three out of four games before we went back into Europe. The only win in that period was the 34–6 victory over Ebbw Vale, although we followed it with bad home defeats to both Newport (31–3) and Neath (32–10). It was tough to take for our fans. Although we started the season pretty well, as it went on we picked up more and more injuries and it became harder and harder to stay competitive. We were down to the bare bones at the club and it was a difficult year.

I didn't play in the Ebbw Vale game or against Newport but returned to the side after the New Year, although things didn't get any better as we lost out in the Celtic League semi-final to Neath 32–10. The Neath defeat, though, was nothing compared to what was about to come with a home defeat to Ulster, 33–21, in the return fixture. We finished off our Heineken Cup campaign by losing in Biarritz.

I missed the Ulster game and was a 61st-minute substitute in France but that hammering from Biarritz will stay with me for a long time. Dai had left Martyn Williams at home for the trip. He said to me that I needed to come into the squad as he had no cover at 10 but there were no plans for me to actually play. Dai was on the bench himself in Biarritz and I remember them getting on a roll which we couldn't stop. They needed 13 tries to qualify for the quarter-finals and they got them.

Incredibly, we were in dreamland early on, a try by Craig Morgan and a seven-point lead inside two minutes being the falsest of dawns as the men from the Basque country gorged themselves on a feast of running rugby. That early deficit was immediately wiped out and by half-time their lead had stretched to 40–13. When we did score early on, I remember they didn't seem that bothered. It certainly didn't faze them as they clearly believed we couldn't hold on. They weren't bothered about defending because it didn't matter how many tries they let in. As long as they won and scored 13 tries, they were through even if they didn't kick conversions.

They got on a roll and we were dropping like flies. There was about 20 minutes to go and only two subs left on the bench, me and Dai Young. Jamie Robinson went down and Dai looked over at me and said, 'It's me or you.' So I got stripped and went on, trying my best to inject some enthusiasm into the defence so we could stem the flow of tries for a few minutes.

Even through those tough times, there were five or six who still regularly played well. The likes of Jamie Robinson, Rhys Williams and Martyn Williams were really digging in but when you aren't retaining possession there is only so much defending you can do. Against Ulster, as against Northampton, Edinburgh, Newport, Neath and countless other opponents that season, the side put their bodies on the line. Seven days after our 75–25 defeat in Biarritz we turned in a four-try-to-one performance to beat Swansea 32–19. I was restored to the number 10 shirt for this game and we came up with the perfect antidote to that trip to France.

I thought I was progressing well but with the new Six Nations championship just around the corner, I was still wondering whether 10 was the best position for me. In the game against Swansea I played well and made a try for Craig Morgan. Generally I didn't have much choice but to play 10 at Cardiff, but I thought 12 was the better option for me. Nicky Robinson was there but Dai Young wanted me to play outside-half. Nicky was 18 or 19 and still learning the game. He was probably a bit too young to play outside-half regularly at that time but now he has developed superbly and turned into a very good player.

If Cardiff had greater resources I think I would have moved to inside-centre much earlier. In fact if Neil Jenkins had still been there I think I would have been playing centre with Neil inside me. I wouldn't have regarded that as any sort of slight. If you are going to run a game from 10 you need to know the game inside out and I was starting to understand that, but there were still things popping up all the time that I had not seen before. I was still learning. I was having really good games but then getting caught out positionally. It was up and down at that stage.

I think it was part of the learning curve you need to go through when you move into a new sport but I also don't think there was anyone at Cardiff who really got hold of me and went through it. I felt there should have been someone there to do that. Unfortunately there wasn't. Cardiff and Wales had invested a lot of money in me and I think, looking back, they could have invested a little more with someone who could have taken me under their wing to explain things. The one person who did help me a lot was Wales coach Steve Hansen. He brought me in for extra video sessions. Although he was national coach he was doing things a national coach wouldn't normally do in spending a lot of time with me and developing me as a player.

We lost 39–26 to Llanelli, undoing some of the good work we had put in against Swansea, and before the end of February I was released from Wales training to play in the 20–20 draw against Neath. The Wales coach Steve Hansen told me that he thought I had been thrown into the deep end internationally and that I needed more time to develop. Steve said he wanted to bring me off the bench and that he felt I needed as much game-time as possible but in the right environment. He was determined to handle it right and said he wanted me playing at the right level and that meant on the bench for Wales and in the starting line-up for Cardiff.

Cardiff may have started the season poorly but you couldn't accuse us of finishing the 2002–03 campaign badly as we picked up 9 wins in our last 11 matches, the final game of the season on 30 May being a 30–21 win over Pontypridd. During that run, I think it was the 28–27 victory at home to Llanelli, who Dai Young acknowledged as the best in Wales, that we were most proud of, although we did put 44 points on Swansea at the start of the run.

Unfortunately one of only two defeats in that period came at the hands of Llanelli in the Welsh Cup semi-final, 44–10 at the Millennium Stadium. We went into the match in high spirits having beaten Pontypridd and Swansea but it wasn't to be against Llanelli. Dai Young said, 'We made far too many mistakes. International players, from whom we would expect better, were at fault and we leaked the first three tries simply because of missed tackles. There was also far too much aimless kicking.' During that run, I was moving from outside-half to centre and back again, so much so that I was the subject of a poll on the Cardiff website. There were almost 500 votes on this subject with 70 per cent saying I should be in the number 12 shirt.

When we beat Newport in April, 39–17, there was a remarkable display by Rhys Williams. Playing at full-back, he scored four of our five tries leading the team out on his 101st appearance.

We played Caerphilly on back-to-back weekends to start May 2003 and in the second fixture I scored a good try and picked up 23 points, converting all six of Cardiff's tries in the 48–32 victory. After our frustrating year, we were determined to finish on a high to set up things for the next season. Those 23 points against

Caerphilly took me past 200 for the season and 400 for the club since my debut 18 months before. Those totals weren't too significant though. As a goalkicker you are always going to pick up points. I was kicking pretty well that year and I saw it as a reasonably successful campaign on a personal level. I managed to push myself into Steve Hansen's plans on a regular basis so it was all starting to come together.

Before regional rugby took off in Wales, we finished off the final Premiership season in style, beating Bridgend 27–13 and Pontypridd 30–21 to finish third in the table. It had been a hard, difficult season playing in a doomed competition. We knew by the end of the season that for the next campaign we would be the Cardiff Blues and the regional set-up in Wales would be launched. Initially, we were told we had to finish in the top four to make it into Europe and then they said it didn't matter as the regions were starting. Nobody really knew what was happening.

That final Bridgend win also marked John Tait's farewell. The Canadian lock, who had spent six years at Cardiff, signed a two-year deal with French club Brive.

John was a real character, a larger than life figure around the club. I was very fond of him but I think John had lost a bit of interest towards the end. He suffered a number of injuries and he was one of the big players who just didn't figure enough times for us. That was Cardiff's story in 2002–03 in many ways. We had some good players but we couldn't get them on the field enough times.

I didn't know when I started the 2003–04 season as a member of the new Cardiff Blues region that it would be my last in union. I was playing in rugby league when it launched the new Super League structure and was moving to becoming a summer sport. When rugby union changed in Wales to a regional structure it took a while to get into the flow of it. It took a while for the game in Wales to improve and I could see it taking three to five years to really kick on. It was a minor factor in my decision to go back to league a year later.

Even now I don't think they've got the structure right. I know everyone is pointing to how strong the national game is with that unforgettable Grand Slam in 2005 but that covered up an awful season for the regions in the Heineken Cup when none of them qualified for the quarter-finals. One minute the club game seems to be going well and then all the players disappear for Wales training. The movement from one competition to another and back again doesn't help.

I couldn't see how they could structure it right. They need to decide what they are going to do. One minute they are pushing all the resources into the regional game and then they are taking the best players away to play for Wales. They are not really consistent in anything they are doing with the regions and it is hurting their development.

One of the main consequences of the move to a regional system was that the club system was moved out of the spotlight. The regions were always going to be in Europe. Qualification changed a little over the ensuing years and after another bad season in 2004–05, Cardiff had to qualify for the Heineken Cup against an Italian side.

I regret the demise of some of the traditional Welsh clubs. The WRU were creating the regions and the Welsh league didn't seem to matter.

There wasn't any relegation so the teams were never worried about dropping down and those in the lower league could never come up into the Celtic League. Even in Super League, although some people oppose it, we have relegation and the same happens in the Zurich Premiership where we saw Harlequins suffer the drop in 2005.

In rugby league, even if you are a top team, when you are going to play one of the sides in the bottom two or three you know you are in for a tough day at the office because of that fear of relegation. You didn't get that with the Welsh regions in the first season and a lot of the games had no atmosphere. The Heineken Cup, which was an outstanding competition, could be just six

151

matches and a lot of the games had nothing counting on them, unlike those international games I played for Wales.

The Welsh-Scottish League became the Celtic League, which in essence was a good idea because it brought cross-border competition. However, in practice even this had its problems as there was a feeling at the start that the Irish teams weren't taking it very seriously and resting their players. This meant playing Irish sides made up of second-team players as the others prepared for either the autumn internationals or the Six Nations. The league became not as serious as it could have been. I think they looked at the Zurich Premiership and felt that that was what they wanted but they didn't know how to get it. The Premiership has been going for quite a long time and the clubs have invested a lot of time and effort into it.

I found it a frustrating time, as no one seemed to know where the Celtic League was going. There was talk of the Irish or the Scottish teams dropping out and I still think, even now, they appear to be a little bit lost. Every season, there appeared to be a new proposal dreamt up for a new competition. I believe they need to agree a structure and then stick to it for, say, eight to ten years before reviewing it.

I didn't have much luck with my summers in rugby union. At the end of the 2002–03 season I had started playing 12 for Wales but suffered a shoulder injury in the last international of the season against the Barbarians and missed what I thought was a massive tour to Australia and New Zealand.

All I was left with was the prospect of making sure I had a big pre-season. The Cardiff Blues kicked off their new existence with a game against Leicester which we lost 23–22. With the World Cup around the corner, I was in camp with Wales at the time of the Leicester game so I wasn't training with the club, but all the Cardiff players in the Welsh squad went along to see the birth of our new team. This was a tough year for the regions, as they had to kick off their new lives without their international players. Perhaps that added to the stilted start.

Club rugby in Wales took a back seat completely. It was difficult to get excited about the domestic game because you knew you weren't going to be involved in it until after you came back from Australia. I didn't see too many differences between Cardiff RFC and the Cardiff Blues. The training facilities certainly stayed the same, the coaching team stayed the same and the playing squad pretty much stayed the same. In contrast, when Warrington turned into Warrington Wolves and Super League started, I saw massive changes. The comparison isn't that fair because before Super League we were part-time, while in Wales the club rugby was already full-time and it went from winter to summer in league.

But in rugby league I still thought they made a bigger effort with their launch. There was a big effort with the marketing to launch it with a bang. In England I thought the transformation to the Zurich Premiership brought other changes but in Wales all they seemed to do was change the names. I know the Welsh Rugby Union were seriously lacking in funds at the time so maybe that was the reason.

After we returned from the World Cup, the Blues went through a torrid time, losing seven successive matches, beginning with our 32–7 Celtic League defeat to Ulster on 31 October and ending with victory over Biarritz in the Heineken Cup in the middle of January. Again, we weren't equipped to perform at that level, so that win over Biarritz was the highlight of our season. Seven days after losing 35–20 to Biarritz over there we beat them 21–20 at Cardiff Arms Park. I remember Dimitri Yachvili missing a simple penalty in front of the posts. Two more set-pieces later, after five minutes of added time, the final whistle went.

The win over Biarritz inspired us to finish our Heineken Cup campaign on a high, running in three tries in a 22–7 victory over Sale at a gale-hit Cardiff Arms Park. Due to the World Cup, my first start for the new Cardiff Blues region came on 28 November in the 31–10 defeat by Munster and I had to wait until the start of April to actually record my first win, the 19–15 victory over

Ulster. That was when I had been switched to inside-centre after playing there in the Six Nations.

In my return Munster game, it was back to outside-half for me from the number 12 shirt I wore at the World Cup. Coach Dai Young explained it by saying, 'I have spoken to Steve Hansen with regards to that. He welcomes the opportunity for Iestyn to play at 10. Although he picks him at 12 there could be occasions when he needs to slot in at fly-half for Wales. From our point of view we signed Iestyn as a 10 and have recruited around him on that basis. If he commits to us long term beyond his contract then perhaps we may have to change our thought process.'

The change of position, playing 10 for Cardiff and 12 for Wales, did take a bit of getting used to. But I was at 10 when I first arrived at Cardiff, so it wasn't that bad. There were some new moves and new calls to learn but I was still confident I could go back to playing there. I remember Dai taking me to one side and explaining that he needed me to slot back into the outside-half role. He said he understood that I wanted to play 12 but he added that he needed me to play 10, saying the time wasn't right for me to move to 12 for Cardiff. I accepted that. When a coach comes to you like that you haven't got much choice and it was a matter of me just getting on with it.

I still had an open mind about returning to league or staying with union after this season. I had really enjoyed the World Cup and the Six Nations was still to come. I was excited about that and getting back to playing for Cardiff.

Coming off a medium high at the World Cup, I was looking forward to my return but a back injury ruined my comeback and I was fluctuating from 10 to 12. I had a back spasm in Biarritz when we competed very well. We gave it a real dig and almost took the spoils. I injured my back in the first minute and was in agony for the whole game. I presumed it was a back spasm but it took a week before I could properly walk again. At this stage there were four weeks to the Six Nations and as the Championship got closer I became more desperate to play.

After the Six Nations, at least I managed to sign off my Cardiff career with a victory, although at the time I had no idea it would be my last match in the famous blue and black shirt. It was the 55–22 win over Edinburgh at Cardiff Arms Park and I was then settled in the number 12 shirt full-time, both for Wales and Cardiff. Nicky Robinson was older and when I came back from the Six Nations, Dai told me he was so impressed with Nicky's form that he was happy for me to play in the centre and let him take the 10 shirt.

We performed together towards the end of the season and Dai thought it could be a powerful partnership. But all thoughts of Nicky and me carrying on that partnership ended in that following summer of 2004 when I finally decided to make my move back to rugby league.

SEVEN

UNION FOR WALES: AT LAST!

WHEN I first spoke to Wales coach Graham Henry about moving from rugby league to rugby union in 2001, he was kind enough to lay out a plan for my introduction to the new game. My only previous rugby union experience was that appearance at the Middlesex Sevens, so although I was bursting to get that Wales shirt on, I was also delighted when he explained that, if things went to plan, I would get a gentle introduction into union.

In the autumn internationals of that year, Wales were due to play Argentina, Tonga and Australia, followed by the 2002 Six Nations campaign which would end with Scotland at home. In my mind, I thought if I made the bench for that last game in March, some six months after my arrival in Cardiff, I would have done very well. On the surface there are many similarities between league and union but I knew how totally different the two games were and that I could never expect to move into international union right from the start.

Graham was heavily involved in the negotiations over my move to union, as this transfer from Leeds would be like no other before. Almost every player who completes a transfer does so from club to club but I was moving from Leeds to a contract with the Welsh Rugby Union, who in turn had negotiated another contract with Cardiff. They would share responsibility, but the deal would be done with the WRU, hence Graham's place at the negotiating table.

In those early talks, he said he was planning to let me settle into the Cardiff team, get some game time in this new sport and start to enjoy it. Once I'd played for Cardiff, he said he'd look at the Wales situation, maybe bringing me in for the autumn internationals but just to train with the squad. If all went well, then perhaps he'd put me on the bench for the Tonga game, as they were clearly the weakest of the three nations Wales were playing in that period, and bring me on for the last ten minutes so I could get a slow introduction to international rugby union.

To me, that sounded perfect as I knew, especially if I was going to play outside half or centre, it would take me some time to settle in. My position was never really an issue in the move, although many people thought it would be better for me to kick off life in union at full-back, slightly out of the spotlight.

The settling-in period was further complicated by the fact that I had the wrist injury which delayed my move into full training a little longer than I would have wanted, although obviously I could still keep my fitness levels up.

Just after I signed, I went to Graham's house, sat down with him and he went through all the moves. At that time things were in a bit of a whirl for me. Graham was talking about the moves and phases and I must admit I didn't understand all of it. He told me that during the up and coming autumn internationals I would be in the camp for three weeks, so I could get used to the squad, the players and the set-up before maybe playing ten minutes of international football.

That all sounded great . . . but (and I suppose you knew there was a 'but' coming) after just 200 minutes of union with Cardiff, I was starting the match against Argentina. This came as something of a shock. It put me more than six months ahead of schedule and I'd done nothing to deserve it. When we were in the negotiations the summer before, if anyone had suggested I would start against Argentina the following November, I would have to have said, 'Hang on a minute, how can that be a good idea?'

I understood why people got carried away at the time. I played my first two games for Cardiff and got man of the match in one, but as I explained earlier, these games were one-offs. I'm sure anyone taking a closer look would realise I wasn't ready for international rugby. How could I be after just 200 minutes playing a new sport? And almost all of those minutes against the same side!

I must admit that after those two games I did have a slight misconception about the way the game was played. I didn't know at the time that games could become so technical. The two I had played for Cardiff, both against Glasgow, were open and exciting but they were totally different to an international match. But because of the way people can get carried away with rugby in Wales no one wanted to listen to the other view, that I wasn't ready for international rugby. Looking back, it was obvious. How could I be?

My advice to any other player following in my footsteps is to take it slowly. Try to make as low-profile a start as possible and take your introduction into international rugby as steadily as possible. I just wanted to get a season under my belt when I might have had a couple of starts and a couple of games on the bench in the Six Nations, maybe pushing for a permanent starting spot in the 2002 autumn internationals. I felt that was the right thing and I believed the WRU thought that as well.

I got picked in the training squad for the autumn internationals in 2001 on the strength of those two games for Cardiff but I wasn't worried. No one told me I might start. I thought we were still on course for me, perhaps, having ten minutes against Tonga.

The media campaign had of course gathered pace by this stage, with people saying I should be started at 10 against Argentina. I took the articles with a pinch of salt as I didn't think I was ready for that and I didn't think anyone else thought I was either. Well, no one apart from Graham Henry anyway!

As much as I admire Andy Farrell and his abilities I hope, for his sake, that the RFU take the Jason Robinson route rather than the Iestyn Harris route for Andy's introduction into international rugby. Like me, he carried out his negotiations with a governing body, the RFU, rather than a club.

The clamour from fans and the media alike is for players like Andy Farrell to start international rugby as soon as they can but they must be resisted. I have no doubt about Andy's abilities and I know he'll make a big success of his union career, but he'll have more chance of success if he is introduced into the Test side slowly. There was talk of him going to the Churchill Cup with England in the summer of 2005 before he had even played a game of union! That was a crazy notion and I'm glad that became no more than a suggestion. If he had, it would have been worse than what happened to me.

Even when I turned up for that first Wales training session, in the week of the Argentina game, I didn't think for one minute that I would be in the starting XV. However, I got into the Wales camp and on the Monday Graham announced, in front of everyone, he was starting me, at outside-half, the following Saturday. He just read it out in a training session at The Barn, our base at The Vale Hotel, near Cardiff. I couldn't really believe it as the names were read out. I felt immensely proud. I had only been playing two weeks of rugby so to get the chance to play for Wales was massive. But when you put it in those terms, two weeks of rugby union before my first cap, it sounds ridiculous.

How could I do anything else but accept? Can you imagine the reaction if I had turned down the chance? Even if Graham had come to me one-on-one and told me he was thinking of picking me at outside-half, I think I would still have gone for it, carried away in the moment, I suppose.

I think it would have been great if he'd come to see me and said, 'I think you have gone really well over the last two games.

What I think I'm going to do is put you on the bench against Argentina.' I would have been happier among the substitutes although to be honest, with the way the game developed, it was so technical that I don't think Graham would have brought me on. Actually, I would have been happy simply with a place in the stand to watch the game and the chance to spend some time with my new teammates. It is one thing to join a new club and then go straight into a match like I had done in rugby league with Leeds, but to go straight into a Test match?

When the chance of playing international rugby union came, part of me was thinking that I should turn it down. But as a sportsman in a physical game like rugby, I knew that my next game could be my last. Also, you must remember that I was being offered the chance to do something I had dreamed about all my life. I just couldn't turn it down. It is hard to be rational when you are offered one of the most famous jerseys in the sporting world – the Wales number 10. That Welsh jersey meant so much to me and was the reason I had moved 'south'. You don't say you don't want to play for your country.

Graham came to both Glasgow games, the second of which was 48 hours before he told me I would make my debut for Wales. He said he thought I was ready and all I could think about was trying to have a low-key week and just getting on with it.

But there was no chance of that, from then on it was a bit of a whirlwind. Everything happened so fast, it just seemed to be press conference after press conference, interview after interview and training session after training session. There certainly wasn't time to talk to anyone about the offer Graham had made, not even to Becky. There was simply no time to even think about it.

You have to remember that all this happened on my first day with the Wales team at the first training session, where I thought I was just going along for the ride and getting a taste of what international rugby union was all about. Part of me thought I could learn as I went along, but how can you do that against a top-class international side like Argentina? The Pumas have been in the top echelons of international rugby for decades. In 1999 they beat Ireland to make the World Cup quarter-finals and in 2005 a third-string side drew with the Lions at the Millennium Stadium.

Graham obviously had great faith in me, which I can only thank him for, but that faith was misguided and, to be honest, I only really found my feet in international rugby union two years later, playing centre at the World Cup.

Looking back, you have to look for other motives for my selection against Argentina, as I can't believe it was just on playing ability. How could it be?

The WRU had paid a big transfer fee for me and the ticket sales for the Argentina game had been slow. Maybe they were looking to recoup some of that transfer fee on ticket sales in this first game? At the end of October, *The Mirror* newspaper reported that 20,000 tickets had been sold for the clash against the Pumas, but they estimated that if I played, it could swell the gate to 60,000, which would have provided an extra £600,000 for the WRU. In the end, 39,000 paid to attend the match.

Obviously I had watched a lot of games and studied the tapes, but I didn't understand some of the basics of the role of an outside-half. I didn't know that if it was slow ball, for example, you can't stand flat, you have to stay in the pocket and maybe kick to the corners. If it's quick ball, you can keep it, but I didn't really understand that at the time.

If you don't grow up with the game or haven't played it for a long time, it is hard to grasp these concepts.

I don't wish, even in hindsight, that I had turned down that chance to play for Wales. But I think it was unrealistic and unfair to expect me to play at 10 in a Test match against Argentina. To make my debut against a side who were technically very good made it an even stranger choice. Their backs are very efficient and they have a great kicking game, allied to one of the best packs of forwards in the rugby world. It was always going to be very different to the two games against Glasgow!

If Graham really wanted to play me, he could have picked me at inside-centre. Stephen Jones could easily have played 10 but instead he ended up lining up outside me. Later in my international career, I was moved to inside-centre, and I don't understand why it didn't happen then. At 12 you get a little more breathing space and they're not asking you to run the game and make the calls.

It wasn't as if Stephen was inexperienced himself. Before that game, he had 21 caps to his name, having made his debut three years earlier. Stephen has proved since what an accomplished outside-half he is, playing a crucial role in Wales's Grand Slam triumph of 2005.

By the time we got to the World Cup, two years after my debut, Stephen was playing outside-half anyway, with me at centre. When it came to the 2005 Lions tour, Stephen's ability was recognised by Clive Woodward who picked him to wear the Lions number 10 shirt, with Jonny Wilkinson moving to inside-centre.

If I had kicked off that way, at centre, I would have been a junior partner in the combination but, and it sounds ludicrous now looking back, I was selected as the senior partner. I could have learned a lot from Stephen at that early stage, but wasn't really given the chance.

That game was something of a nightmare for me and I suppose I could have predicted it. I really didn't know what I was doing. It wasn't so much the laws, I could learn them, but I didn't know when to kick or pass or where to pass. That sort of decision-making comes with experience. I often just threw out a long pass because it was the only thing I could think to do.

In the build-up to the game, as if I didn't have enough pressure on my shoulders, the comparisons with the great Welsh halves of previous eras started: players I had heard about in the bedtime stories from my dad; players who had grown up in union and who were immersed in the game before they made their Wales debuts.

By the time the game arrived, the interest in me was huge. It went completely over the top and was out of all proportion.

Preparing for my first cap, I was far more nervous than normal, certainly more than when I had played for Wales or Great Britain at league. I suppose my body was dropping a few hints for me. The build-up felt very strange and to experience it for the first time as a starting player was very hard.

It would have been nice to just stay in the hotel, attend the team talks, complete the training, enjoy the big day and take part in everything from being on the bus, with a police escort, to singing the national anthem – but without the pressure of actually playing at the end of it. I never got that sort of luxury; instead, I went on a very steep learning curve.

Argentina had such a big, aggressive pack that a lot of our play was in and around the rucks. It was tight. Now, if I played at 10, in a similar game, I would keep it tight but at the time my instincts were to run and pass, though clearly this wasn't the right game to do that.

The nerves I had before the Argentina game disappeared as soon as the whistle went and I settled down. The space was there for me, but the possession wasn't. We didn't have much possession and lost a lot of ball up front. We were unable to play the game we wanted. We didn't get the quality ball that we hoped for, were under pressure and could not turn it around. Argentina achieved their first win over Wales in six fully fledged Tests.

The game was described in *The Independent*:

> Argentina handled Harris cleverly. In attacking positions they stood off him, for fear of committing men to his devilish turn of foot. Far too often for Wales's liking, Harris was on the end of painfully slow ball and the blue and white hoops were on him in droves, forcing embarrassing charge-downs. Scott Quinnell was an exception but his charges were too few and far between.

I think I coped but playing that first game at 10 was just too much. Wales were booed off following that 30–16 defeat, hardly the sort of introduction to my career in international rugby union I had planned. I had to keep telling myself this would have been a tough game whoever was at 10. Argentina have such an aggressive style, they tie people up at the ruck and drop two or three players really deep to catch the kicks.

If their forwards get on top, they are a difficult team to play against and that day they were physically dominant. We had a tough day at the scrums and the rucks and there weren't too many places to put the ball.

They dominated our pack and everyone knows it is tough to win under those circumstances. Rob Howley was struggling to box kick as he was getting scrappy ball, so he had no choice but to pass it to me. At that time I wasn't aware I needed to drop deep. In the Cardiff games Rob could protect me a little more but against Argentina he didn't have time to set himself. He was doing his best to look after me but he was under so much pressure himself he couldn't do as much as he would have wanted to. I suppose the low point came late on when I had a kick charged down which they scored off. After that we were never in it and were chasing the game the whole of the second half, trying things we wouldn't normally try, most of which didn't come off.

After the game everyone was upset. I had to do a press conference and explain that I was on a steep learning curve and that I had to ride the ups and downs. The week after, the Pumas went to Scotland and won 25–16, following that up with a narrow defeat against the All Blacks, which proved what a good team they were.

Obviously, you don't imagine that your first appearance for Wales will go the way it did for me. It was disappointing, but I picked myself up quickly.

Many people think it would have been hard coming into that Cardiff dressing-room with that big transfer fee or coming straight into the Wales team with just a couple of games under my belt but I had absolutely no problems in either dressing-room and the players could not have done any more for me.

Rob looked after me the day after the Argentina game. Great Britain were playing Australia in rugby league and he suggested we go and have a drink and watch it together, just to get away from everything. At the time it was perfect for me.

I went with him and Gareth Thomas to a rugby club in Bridgend and we had a really good day, having a drink and watching the match. I remember we ended up getting really drunk, despite the fact we had training on the Monday.

Rob kept saying we'd be OK but we turned up feeling very rough. As I ran out, I saw him on the physio's bench. I said, 'You not training?' He replied, 'No, I've got a bad knee.' I was totally stitched up!

The crowd were also very supportive in that Argentina game and I thank them for that. I know they booed the team at the end but they did all they could to lift me. I think they were frustrated as they could see we were on the back foot.

Graham spoke to me after the match and said he was going to move me to inside-centre for the next game, that 10 was too technical a position. If only he'd said that a week earlier! Although I wouldn't have wanted to wear the English jersey that Jason has worn with such awesome effect, I would certainly have swapped my introduction to union for his. Who knows if doing it England's way would have made a difference to my union career? We'll never know.

After the Argentina defeat, we learnt about the retirement of Dai Young, another former rugby leaguer, Scott Quinnell, taking over the captaincy from him.

Dai didn't talk to me about it before, he simply felt the time was right. Just before Dai quit, Steve Hansen had come in to work with Graham, as his assistant, and he brought a new way of thinking with him.

In the autumn internationals, Steve came to me and said, 'Do you know how to place the ball after a tackle?' I had to admit I didn't. I was playing international rugby and didn't know one of the basics. Steve spent about half an hour with me and a tackling shield, taking me through some drills. He was the first person to get hold of me and explain the technique and that was after I had made my Test debut.

I enjoyed the experience of playing for Wales, of course I did. I obviously made some mistakes but that's why I was desperate to play in the next match, against Tonga, and put things right. The Argentina game made me all the more determined to get back out there for Wales and prove my worth. I was serving my apprenticeship in union and people will say I should not have played again but I wanted to get out there and start the learning process. I was in the public eye and everything I did was under the microscope but I knew I had to knuckle down and get on with the job.

Things did get better as we were able to gain some pride back with a 51–7 win over Tonga. For that game, I switched positions with Stephen Jones, moving from outside-half to inside-centre. Luckily, the Tonga game was far more open, and I kicked five penalties and converted three of our tries. If you are playing poorly, it shouldn't mean you kick poorly, so I didn't expect my struggles on the field to affect the way I kicked.

It was great playing outside Stephen Jones. Like Rob at Cardiff, Stephen did a great job looking after me against Tonga and the next one against Australia. He released the ball to me when it could be released and when it couldn't he'd put it in the corner, which worked well, especially against Tonga.

That was followed by another baptism of fire for me as we welcomed the reigning world champions, Australia, to Cardiff. People were predicting Australia would put 50 points on us but that performance showed the character of our side. Of course we had a lot of defending to do, as you can imagine against a side that had just beaten the Lions, but I think we did it well. We suffered a 21–13 defeat but we did manage to score the final try of the game. In the end it wasn't too bad and I think the team had got back some of the pride we'd lost against Argentina.

John Eales, the great Australian second row and World Cup-winning captain, expressed surprise at my rapid promotion, comparing my introduction to union with that of league stars Mat Rogers and Wendell Sailor, who made the same move in Australia, with a view to playing in the 2003 World Cup. Eales said, 'I don't think it would have happened straight away in Australia. The policy has been clear since we've signed the likes of Wendell Sailor and Mat Rogers. They have to earn their way into the Test team. In Australia, it would probably mean playing most of the Super 12 season to be in with a chance of being selected. He would have to earn his place ahead of the player that has been playing and training and earning that spot over the last year or whatever. It's the finer points that won't come naturally to someone who hasn't played the game for a long time. It's going to be a huge challenge for him to get to Test standard in a sport he has basically never played before.'

We all went for a meal together with our wives after the game against Australia and there was a general feeling of contentment in the squad. Of course we'd never settle for a defeat but after the loss to Argentina it was important we got some pride back, which we did against the Wallabies. We felt we had made progress in the autumn series and that was the important thing.

After Christmas, it was time for me to start the first Six Nations Championship of my career. I was at inside-centre for our first game, against Ireland at Lansdowne Road, and although we didn't go into the game lacking confidence, we ended up getting thumped 54–10, Ireland taking us apart completely.

Stephen had kicked everything in sight for Llanelli, so Graham said we'd keep him kicking, which I didn't mind. I watched some of the Llanelli games and could only agree. After that defeat, I had a feeling on the way home that Graham wouldn't coach us again. The game had gone so badly that when we got to the airport there were thousands of Welsh fans and they were heckling us and saying we were the worst team in the world. Graham got a lot of flak and on that journey home he looked really depressed and ready for a change.

We had a feeling he was going to quit and when we came into training on the Monday he had resigned, with Steve Hansen taking over. Graham Henry was such a big supporter of my move to union that it was a blow to my ambitions to see him resign after the Ireland game. His departure put me in a state of flux and one of the first things the new coach, Steve Hansen, did was to pull me into his office and tell me he was going to put me on the bench for the home game against France. He said that he wanted to take me out of the limelight as he thought I was under too much pressure.

Steve felt I had not been treated in the right way and he said he wanted to bring me in slowly over the course of the Six Nations. He said he knew I wouldn't be happy with his decision but he concluded by saying he was going to do what was best for the team, which meant picking Stephen at 10 and Andy Marinos of Newport outside him.

Although I was frustrated, I just had to accept it and get on with it. I knew that starting on the bench was probably the best thing as I had so much to learn. Still, I was disappointed because no player wants to be left out of any team. I was good friends with Andy, so I wished him all the best for the game. I had the choice of sulking and going away or getting on with it and trying to learn as much as possible, which is what I decided to do.

Looking back, sitting on the bench for the visit of France in the Six Nations was exactly where I should have been in my rugby development but obviously after having started in the four internationals before, dropping down was hard to take.

I wasn't too worried, however, because Steve Hansen was bringing me on as a player and he kept reminding me that the World Cup was 18 months away, and that tournament was my target. Steve said he wanted me to go on a curve upwards rather than one that was like a roller-coaster ride. It was frustrating for me at the time but, looking back, it was the right thing to do.

I didn't get on against France, even though I thought I could have done something in those last 10 or 20 minutes. I spoke to

Steve at the after-match function and he told me I had to bide my time and that he felt it wasn't the right game for me to come into.

That wasn't the case against Italy as I came on at full-back, replacing Kevin Morgan with 20 minutes to go and I think I did a few decent things in the game, which we won 44–20. Although I was a little bit lost at full-back, I definitely thought I was making progress, so perhaps Steve's strategy with me was working. Steve actually apologised for throwing me in at full-back after the game but he explained he had little choice after Kevin went down.

He said he was always going to put me on and afterwards he said he should have shuffled a few more players and slotted me in at centre. Dafydd James and Rhys Williams were the wings on that day and they did what they could to help me, Rhys telling me when to push up or pull back.

Steve Hansen had planned to continue my slow integration into the team but an injury to Stephen Jones before our next game, against England, changed that. Stephen hadn't recovered from back spasms and Steve Hansen had called me and said he was impressed with the way I had gone against Italy and that he believed I had turned the corner. I was back at outside-half for my first Six Nations start at Twickenham. That pep talk gave me a big boost and even though we got badly beaten, I thought I had a reasonable game, scoring a try, a penalty and a conversion. At that time, England were building into World Cup-winning mode but we competed with them in major aspects of the game. I thought we performed reasonably well as a team and made two or three breaks.

After the game, I got a chance to catch up with Phil Larder, my old Great Britain rugby league coach, and Dave Alred, my old kicking coach.

Phil was very important to me in my league career, rescuing me from the bad days at Warrington by taking me on my first GB tour. Phil was kind to me that day at Twickenham, explaining that it would take time for me to learn union, and that I should be patient.

It was the first time I had seen Dave Alred since I was 16. I didn't think for one moment Dave would remember me, but he did. He was a nice man in that week at Warrington, when I was first introduced to goalkicking, and he came over and spoke to me at Twickenham, wishing me well for the future.

The 2002 Six Nations ended on a real downer as we lost our final game 27–22 at home to Scotland, going down to two very late penalties. I did manage to get involved in a try for Rhys Williams after coming off the bench.

At the end of my first full season, one player who knew exactly what I was going through was Jason Robinson. He had also switched from union to league but had a very different introduction to the England team and top-level rugby union than I did. He said in *Wales on Sunday*,

Iestyn has been thrown in at the deep end, and it has not helped him one bit. When I saw how early he was put into the Wales team, I was surprised and I knew it was going to be tough for him.

No disrespect, but the Welsh team has not been playing well and if you haven't got the players around you playing with confidence you will not be able to do anything.

The union switch has been outstanding for me, but I was introduced slowly with substitute appearances, just having 20 minutes here and there.

I wasn't thrown in before I could swim. Some people would do well to remember that union is a lot different to league. There are so many things Iestyn would have had to get to grips with in a short space of time, especially playing outside-half. And surprise, surprise, there are always plenty of people ready to knock him.

Iestyn will not get any better until the Welsh team starts to get better. If you don't have the runners around you, you will struggle, no matter who you are. I have hardly spoken to Iestyn since I made the switch. But it would be nice to catch up with him and compare notes because of the respect I have for him.

I could have joined Jason in that England team, which finally won the World Cup in 2003, but in the end there was no decision to be made. When Clive Woodward heard that I was probably heading to rugby union, he phoned me around four times with a view to try and make me pick England rather than Wales. Being born in England, I would have had no trouble qualifying for them. I presume I would then have been settled with a union club like Leeds or Sale, with Jason, and slowly brought into the England set-up.

But in the end I never even returned Clive's calls. I hope he never thought I was being disrespectful or rude but I knew there was no point even starting the conversation because although I qualified for England, on residential grounds, I was never going to play for them. The only country I was ever going to play for was Wales, so there was really no point in starting a discussion with Clive as it would only have gone one way. In 2001, there was even some suggestion that myself and Keiron Cunningham would be invited to play for England at rugby league, should they line up a Test series against the visiting Australians but I rejected it out of hand. I regarded that as ridiculous and I said at the time I definitely wouldn't be turning out for any England side. I think if you'd asked any of the Welsh players who played in the World Cup, they wouldn't want to play for England either.

At the time they (England) were our dreaded enemies. Moving from club to club is one thing but country to country? That wasn't for me. I know my northern accent suggests otherwise but I am Welsh to the core and perhaps it was Clive Griffiths who summed it up best when he said, 'Iestyn is shamelessly Welsh, which most people wouldn't believe just because he has a Lancashire accent.

'His sister is Rhiain and her children are Dewi and Emrys, they are red through and through.'

However, it was never going to be easy for me to make my mark in the Welsh rugby union team. Neil Jenkins, the player I followed into the Wales number 10 shirt, explained how hard it would be for me to meet the expectations of a nation. Speaking on BBC Radio Wales's *The Back Page* programme, Neil summed it up:

> There must be something wrong with us to put all that pressure on one number, one player. It has never changed for as long as I can remember, probably from the 1950s up to now. That's the pressure that the players have to get used to. I tried to accept it, although it was difficult. I just tried to switch off.

The defeat by England was followed by the announcement that Steve Hansen would get the Wales job full time, at least until the end of the 2003–04 season. One thing that I, and the rest of the squad that worked under him, will never forget is his discipline. He was a man of strong character and if you stepped out of line you were out, there was no question about that.

Steve didn't seem interested in the older players and, with an eye on the World Cup, it looked to me that he set about pushing them out so he could bring in the younger players. His attitude was very harsh on the older players in the squad. I thought Scott Quinnell still had a lot to give to Wales when he retired in 2002 and I certainly think Rob Howley did. Ultimately Steve's way provided dividends and we ended up with a good World Cup campaign but I couldn't see why he didn't want those older players involved, particularly Rob. In 2002 Dwayne Peel wasn't ready to take over that number 9 jersey, Gareth Cooper was in there but both could have done with having Rob around. Who wouldn't? I think he asked too many young players to come in and do jobs they had not done before. It was a tough ask of them at that time.

Steve made it clear in that 2002 Six Nations campaign that the next two years were going to be a very tough time, physically and mentally, as we built for the World Cup.

As soon as he took over, he toughened the training up and only wanted his brand of player. Steve's influence even stretched to stopping us playing cards when we were in camp.

Graham Henry, who'd had a fair bit of success, was happy as long as things were all right on the pitch. But Steve wanted everything done his way and he didn't seem to care who he upset. The senior players were saying, 'We don't need this.'

I felt Steve talked down to me a bit because he was that sure about the way he wanted to go. It was bordering on arrogance but, looking back, he needed to be like that. The success the Wales team had in 2005 started with the Hansen era and the work that was put in then. The things he implemented at that time bore fruit when Wales won the Grand Slam. He didn't care how it got done, or who he upset, he just wanted it done the right way. His attitude was that if players weren't up to it or didn't like it, then they should step aside.

His personality changed a lot in the 2003 World Cup, as by then he had the team he wanted and had pushed out those he didn't. It was noticeable how different a bloke he was in Australia. The sessions became short and sharp and if you were feeling a bit drained he might drop the sessions down. Whether that was the plan he had in place from the start, it is difficult to tell. Perhaps, as nothing was expected of Wales at that World Cup and Steve was leaving the job at the end of the tournament, he relaxed a little.

But back in 2002 a lot of players were thinking, 'What have we let ourselves in for?' Steve upset so many players but he didn't care. He used to say, 'If you don't want to be a part of my system, then don't be a part of it.' He told us he had 25,000 Welsh players to pick from and he'd pick one of them if we couldn't handle it.

After that Six Nations, Wales went on a two-Test tour of South Africa but I was forced to miss it. I had a groin injury that had been niggling me for some time and I didn't think I could cope with the hard grounds in South Africa. It would have been too much and once again it was very disappointing not to go away with Wales, as it would not only have given me the chance of picking up some great experience, playing the Springboks in their own backyard, but I would have spent some quality time with the coaches and players.

When the injury first developed, it was taking me 10 to 15 minutes of warming up on my own before I could get moving. I couldn't kick a ball without that warm-up and towards the end of the season, through the Six Nations, it was taking me about 20 or 30 minutes to warm up!

Steve Hansen wanted me on the tour but he said it was crucial that we did what was right for me as he needed me to be 100 per cent for the following year and the World Cup. I went on holiday with Becky and Catrin that summer to get a complete rest. We managed to pick up a last-minute holiday and I ended up watching the games in a bar in the sun as Wales turned in two excellent performances.

In the first Test, in Bloemfontein, I was convinced they were going to go on to win after dominating the opening half-hour and scoring the game's first try after just eight minutes through Craig Morgan. South Africa finally got on top, going on to win 34–19, but that performance showed that Wales were moving in the right direction after a disappointing Six Nations.

The second game was similar in that, once again, Wales gave a great account of themselves. Although they lost 19–8 in Cape Town, the boys knew that if they'd had the bounce of the ball here and there, they could have been celebrating their first win on South African soil.

At the time, the Springboks were in the middle of a reshuffle, so it was a good time to tour there, although it was still a very tough trip. It was very frustrating not to be part of it and, speaking to a few players when they came back, they confirmed what I knew, that the players had no time off and, in the words of one, 'got flogged'. But that's the way Steve Hansen was.

I was a little more established when it came to the 2002 autumn internationals. Well, at least I had some idea about what I was doing! It was still a tough time with Wales, as the losing run was now stretching out behind us, the second South Africa defeat making it one win in eight games.

Before my international season started, I could feel Steve Hansen was taking more and more of an interest in me. He was the guy who spent most time with me. He sat me down and said, 'What do you actually know about rugby union?' I said, 'Very little, really.' I only started improving and getting better consistently when he came in, which I appreciate to this day.

He used to put videos of me and Andrew Mehrtens, the New Zealand fly-half, on at the same time. When I received a ball, he would pause it and say, 'What are you going to do here?' I'd say, 'This, this and this,' and he'd go, 'Fine.' Then he'd play a tape which showed Mehrtens, pause it and say, 'Is that the right option?' I'd reply, 'Yes.' Then he'd say, 'Would you have done that?' I'd reply, 'Well, perhaps no.' Sometimes I'd be in a room with him for two hours and maybe go through just ten minutes of tape because he would keep stopping it.

I came on so much in a period of about two months because of that. That should have happened at the start and it never did, which was frustrating. Each week, he would go through the videos, showing me different games I had played in and some I hadn't. He broke the game down in an interesting way and I even used to take tapes home to study them. It got me thinking about the different ways I could operate on the field.

Neil Jenkins played in our first game of the autumn series, a 40–3 win over Romania, his last cap, although he did come on for a cameo performance at the end of the season against the Barbarians. When the autumn series began in earnest, we managed to silence a few of our growing band of critics with a 58–14 win over Fiji, scoring seven tries under the closed roof at the Millennium Stadium. The boys turned in a display of counter-attacking at pace, built on a fierce defensive display. I only got 30 minutes at the end. I wanted to play, so I wasn't entirely happy with just 30 minutes here and there, but Steve was adamant that the World Cup was his aim for me and he would do anything between these games and the trip to Australia to get me right for that tournament. Steve said that he felt I would be ready to be a major player and a major starter come the World Cup, but at this time he thought I still had a lot to learn. He didn't want me learning the game on the international stage and I couldn't disagree.

A week after the Fiji game, the visitors to Cardiff were Canada, the team we'd have to play in the World Cup in a year's time, so a victory was vital. We knew how important it was to get an edge over them even 12 months before. As Dai Young had retired from international rugby a year earlier, so Scott Quinnell decided this was time for him to go. He came into the game after 56 minutes and received a standing ovation. We won 32–21 with tries from Robin McBryde and Jamie Robinson.

I was on the bench again when we took on New Zealand in the final game of the series, this time at outside-half for Stephen Jones. Jamie Robinson scored a great opening try and we started to believe we could hold on for our first win over the men in black since 1953. But New Zealand had other ideas. I came on with about 30 minutes left and we nearly scored straight away. They replied with a lucky score to push them 14 points ahead but then they pulled away, scoring four second-half tries, including two from Doug Howlett.

I really enjoyed the game and afterwards Steve Hansen pulled me in and said he was really pleased with my progress and that I was getting closer to a starting spot. He didn't waste time taking me through the things I hadn't done that well on the video. I thought there was starting to be a method to what he was doing with me. I was beginning to enjoy my role as an impact player off the bench: it was exciting coming on and trying to spark the team up.

In many ways, Steve Hansen delivered the start I wanted to my

Wales career but it came one year into it! It would have been so much better for me if it had been like this 12 months before. I was getting more comfortable in the games for both Cardiff and Wales. Obviously, I wanted to start more games but Steve was right to leave me on the bench.

We began the 2003 Six Nations with one of Wales's worst defeats in decades, losing 30–22 against Italy in Rome, a scoreline that was only helped by a Dwayne Peel try in the dying minutes. Even though we were on the wrong end of only Italy's second Six Nations win ever, on a personal level it was significant for me, as I started for the first time in almost a year.

In the week leading into the game, we were practising moves from lineouts. I remember speaking to some of the players and they were shaking their heads in disbelief at what Steve Hansen was asking them to do. On defensive lineouts, we were throwing three pods up, a very risky strategy. If we won the ball, fantastic, but if we lost it, Italy were away, as we had no cover from the back of the lineout. I think we won only one of these lineouts in the entire game.

Clive Woodward is a great coach but the key to his success was the way he surrounded himself with other experts. I think, at that time, Steve could have done with surrounding himself with some of those experts, bringing them in to help with areas like the lineout. But he didn't have that back-up and players who know lineouts inside out were just shaking their heads.

We also changed the defence system going into the game after Clive Griffiths had been pushed out, before he was recalled in the Mike Ruddock era and had a big part to play in the 2005 Grand Slam.

Steve changed almost everything for that game, it was bizarre. We were losing ball on first and second phase, we were getting crucified in the lineouts and there were spaces all over the field. It was one of those games where the plan simply didn't work.

We led 17–14 after half an hour and should have taken the game on. What Italy did was use their territory so well. We had the ball for one or two phases and if we had held on to it for five or six phases I believe we would have put 50 points on them. However, we just couldn't. They were getting the ball back, getting a roll on, and we couldn't compete with that.

After the game, Steve didn't acknowledge he'd made any tactical errors. His reaction to the defeat was to give us the longest day of our lives on the Monday in The Barn at the Vale Hotel. He had the forwards doing lineouts for about an hour and the backs tackling for the same amount of time. It was the longest session I'd ever had in my life and I was black and blue. I think everybody was.

In response to that defeat, he made a number of changes for the arrival of England in Cardiff, significantly dropping me back to the bench, which I was annoyed about. He used two or three players as the reason for our awful defeat in Rome but I think it was more to do with the way we were asked to play.

That was a very tough time for me as Ceri Sweeney was moved into the number 10 shirt with Gareth Thomas outside him at inside-centre. I also didn't agree with Steve Hansen's decision to drop our hooker, Mefin Davies, and bring in Jonathan Humphreys, who hadn't played international rugby for more than three years. He also made him captain.

I have nothing against Jonathan, but he hadn't been involved with the squad and many of the players thought it was a backward step. Jonathan was just doing what he was asked to do, and who would turn down being captain of Wales? However, when he called us all in as captain, many of us thought, 'What's happening here?'

Of course we needed a big performance against England but, as Steve had pointed out many times, the World Cup was our objective, so how could bringing Jonathan in, as captain, help that? We had done so much hard work in the last six months, including being flogged, and then to see Jonathan come in just wasn't right.

People like Rob Howley and Scott Quinnell had retired but

then Steve brings in Jonathan Humphreys. We couldn't even work out how he had seen Jonathan play. He wouldn't have seen him play for Wales, or probably for Bath, so it led us to believe that there was someone behind the scenes prompting Steve, but nobody knew who.

The game was built up as a certain 50-pointer but England just didn't play, or rather they played to a very conservative game plan. Jonathan did something to stir up the supporters and I suppose a 26–9 defeat was a partial success. But it was only ever going to be short-term – in fact, he only lasted one more game, leading the side again against Ireland.

I got about 20 minutes at the end of the England game at a time when I thought I was ready to start, so it was beginning to get a bit frustrating again.

I stayed on the bench for the next game, against Scotland, which many thought was our best chance of victory as we had to go from there to play Ireland and France. Again I came on with 30 minutes to go when we were 20 points down. We certainly rallied in the second half, and claimed two consolation tries at the death, but it was a case of too little, too late. We ended up losing 30–22 and it was frustrating for me as I wanted more time. I felt I could have done a lot.

The defeat at Murrayfield left us very deflated, so perhaps it is all the more remarkable that we turned in a good performance in our next game, against Ireland. Before that match, we went down to Tenby in West Wales to train and I remember the last ball session before the game was the worst session I can remember. It was designed so the 15 who were due to start against Ireland played against the eight others, which included me, and we ended up beating them. After the game, people talked about that session and laughed.

Unusually, I was brought on at 12 with Stephen Jones playing at outside-half. I enjoyed that game, perhaps like no other for Wales, as I threw the ball about well and created space and opportunities. It was an unforgettable match, if only for the way it ended, Stephen Jones kicking a late drop goal to put us ahead before Ronan O'Gara landed one for Ireland in injury time to win it. One of the greatest games in Six Nations history, well certainly one of the most exciting!

We weren't far away in that game and in others, so although we were losing, the squad felt we were building and progressing. After that Ireland game, we knew we had the ability to compete at the World Cup.

We finished off our doomed 2003 Six Nations campaign in France, again with me restored to the starting line-up after what I thought was a good half against Ireland. Stade de France was a tough place to make my first start in the Six Nations since we played in Rome and I think they still had a chance of winning the title.

Again we started well but France were always as solid as a rock and eventually got on top. Thomas Castaignède, Vincent Clerc and Frederic Michalak ran in tries in their 33–5 victory, their first over Wales at the stadium. They missed out on the Six Nations title – it went to England who won in the final round against Ireland in Dublin – but they had handed us our first wooden spoon in eight years.

France were always physically dominant and that was a big disappointment. We looked at that game and said we must get to that physical condition and that's when the training increased. Andy Hore, our new fitness coach, became more and more influential in our preparation.

The criticism rained down on me in that Six Nations so it was a huge boost to receive encouragement from one of Wales's greatest outside-halfs, Phil Bennett, out of the blue. Phil, a member of the Wales team who won the Triple Crown three years in succession in the 1970s, gave me his support saying, 'When Iestyn played his first game for Cardiff at Stradey Park, he lit up a moderate game to standards I hadn't seen for years. The following Saturday he scored three tries against Glasgow. They couldn't lay a hand on him. I was the first to urge them to get him into the

Welsh team, but what I hadn't realised was his kicking wasn't quite up to scratch.

'And that's what Iestyn's had to learn, and it's taken him a fair while. I know we spent a lot of money on Iestyn and I know it's been difficult, but I pray that he's still got time left to make an impression. There's been a lot of talk of moving him to another position but he loves fly-half. If he doesn't see the ball for half-an-hour he'll be thinking, "What am I doing here?" so he wants to be part of the action and number 10 is the obvious position.

'I just hope we see the best of him, because there's genius in him. But it's always difficult when you're in a side that's struggling to get results.'

This was the championship when I really made the move from outside-half to inside-centre. I was coming off the bench and played at 12 from the start against France, while still playing 10 for Cardiff.

In the summer of 2003, Wales went to New Zealand and Australia, as did England, but with far worse results, losing 55–3 to New Zealand and 30–10 to Australia. I was really looking forward to this tour, as I believed I was developing on the international stage as an inside-centre. But at the end of the season we played the Barbarians and I injured the ligaments in my shoulder in the last ten minutes of the game. Neil Jenkins, in his swansong, came on for me.

I think any Welshman in the world has respect for Neil Jenkins, as he has done so much for rugby union in Wales. It was a privilege to be involved in his last international match with one of the legends of the game. He had a mini-resurgence trying to get back into the shake-up for the World Cup but I think he realised the physical demands, given he had a serious knee injury, prevented him making a real challenge. I think he realised it wasn't meant to be and at the Barbarians game everyone said goodbye to him, which was a great way to go out. He came on in the 66th minute for his 100th and final Welsh appearance and kicked the last points of the game with a late conversion.

The day after that Barbarians game, I had to go and see the surgeon and he said, 'I need to do a bit of work in there so if you go on tour and you get another knock it could be a reconstruction of the shoulder.'

I was devastated. This was a massive tour. I just wanted to be involved in it and was thinking of ignoring the surgeon's advice, hoping it would be OK. I went to see Steve Hansen and he said that although it was an important tour we had the World Cup in a few months and it simply wasn't worth the risk. He told me to rest up and have a good pre-season, which I did. However, before I began my recuperation I became embroiled in one of the most bizarre episodes of my life. Before the squad got on the plane to go Down Under there was a dispute with the WRU over the players' bonuses for matches.

I was stuck in the middle because I was the only one who had a contract directly with the WRU and wasn't allowed to get involved. The rest of the players were taking a stand as they had seen their match fees come down over the few seasons before.

There seemed to be the understanding that a few years earlier the money was exaggerated and needed to come down, although the players believed the reductions had gone too far. In the end, the money was ridiculously low compared to other nations in the world of rugby. The players said they had to take a stand and even if they didn't get an increase they thought it was worth making the point to ensure it didn't continue in a downward spiral.

This was talked about in the weeks leading into the tour and certainly at the Barbarians game. I didn't actually pull out of the tour until the day of departure, the same day the players had decided to draw a line in the sand. I went to see Steve Hansen at The Vale to tell him I wasn't fit enough to travel and Steve said, 'Where are the players?', to which I could only answer, 'I don't know.' He said I was lying. I had to admit, I did know. They were at the service station near The Vale. I told Steve I wasn't telling him because the boys were taking a stand, and although I couldn't get involved myself, I agreed with the stance they were taking.

Then a message came through that they had been spotted at the service station. Well it's hard for about 40 rugby players to stay incognito for too long! I drove to the service station to tell them they had been seen and that it was only a matter of time before the press turned up. I said they needed to get away from there to somewhere more discreet, and gave them my best wishes before I left.

The delay meant they missed their plane to New Zealand, which was clearly embarrassing for the WRU. Eventually they did leave, although not until the players had accepted a new, revised pay deal. The vote was something like 17–14 in favour of going, so they were close to not making the tour at all. Up until that point, there had been no negotiations between the players and the WRU, so I don't think they had much choice but to make a stand.

For that trip, Steve Hansen took the unique step of naming four tour skippers in his 30-man squad: Martyn Williams, Colin Charvis, Robin McBryde and Stephen Jones.

That idea didn't last long. It was a little bit bizarre and no one really understood what the four captains concept was all about. Obviously you need leaders all over the pitch but I believe you still need one captain.

If anyone was in any doubt about how Steve saw me, he told the media after announcing the squad for that summer tour, 'We see Iestyn Harris playing in the utility role and, if we are going to play him at 12, we have to see him as much as we can. But we will see Iestyn at 10 again because in the modern game you need two outside-halves on the park and he has the ability to give us that.'

As I was injured, Becky, Catrin and I headed to Minorca to watch the matches against New Zealand and Australia in a bar but they were games I didn't relish watching. Wales went there without much confidence after that Six Nations and, with the games being pretty much back-to-back, I knew it would be difficult.

There was no doubt it was a very tough tour. They struggled in the two Tests and I think what made it harder was that England were over there doing very well by beating both New Zealand and Australia. The bar in Minorca was heaving when England were playing, and winning, and then it would empty when Wales were on, just me in there with a cup of coffee.

The World Cup put everyone in Welsh rugby on a high going into the 2004 Six Nations but everyone in the squad knew we'd proved nothing until we had beaten one of the big teams. We all knew this was also Steve Hansen's last tournament before he returned to New Zealand, as there was nothing to indicate, despite a good World Cup, that he was going to change his mind about leaving.

The 2004 tournament kicked off well and we almost picked up where we left off in the World Cup in our opening game against Scotland. We turned in a great attacking performance, playing with real flair, and scored some great tries, Rhys Williams getting two, prop Adam Jones romping home from 30 yards and Stephen Jones kicking eight points in our 23–10 victory. The bulging discs in my back that kept me out of action for Cardiff at the turn of the year certainly got tested 15 minutes from the end when I was hit by Jason White! Despite that, I felt pretty good and I knew the injury was behind me.

We promised so much that year but after the euphoria of the Scotland win we ended up getting thumped by Ireland in the next round, 36–15. With the wind at their backs, Ireland scored four tries before half-time and blew us away. Two late tries from one of Wales's new stars, Tom Shanklin, gave the scoreline a hint of respectability.

Our disappointing Six Nations continued with France at home, a match we lost 29–22. It was a close game but we never really performed in the way we had in Australia a few short months before. We had one try disallowed, which would have put us ahead, but they showed what a good side they were by winning that day and going on to take the Grand Slam in 2004. They had lost to England in the semi-final of the World Cup and they were

185

still bitter about that, wanting to do all they could to make up for it. Well, make up for it in the Six Nations anyway.

We didn't get a lot of quality ball that day and gave away too many turnovers, so it was a difficult game to get into. It was one of those days when the calls go against you, although I was in disbelief when we had our second-half try disallowed for crossing. The French had got away with exactly the same sort of move in the first half!

I missed the England game at Twickenham with a knee injury that would eventually cause me to miss the summer tour to Argentina. Tom Shanklin came in and played really well and the world champions were given a major scare as we fought back from 16–9 down to take a 21–16 lead, before eventually losing 31–21, our best result there since 1986.

After missing the England match, I was desperate to play against Italy, especially after what they had done to us in Rome a year earlier. But I knew I had only a 50:50 chance as Tom had played so well against England. I had a fitness test the day before the game and Steve Hansen told me that although I was starting, he would probably give Tom around 20 minutes, irrespective of how the game was going, as he was in such good form.

When you come off with 20 minutes to go you don't expect to get the man-of-the-match award, but I took the champagne home and put it on ice! We'd done a lot of the donkey work in the first 60 minutes and when I came off the game opened up, and we went on to win 44–10.

It was a very special day for Gareth Thomas as he scored his 34th try to beat Ieuan Evans' Wales try-scoring record.

Everyone wanted to put in a big performance for Steve Hansen to show the extent of his achievements in his two years in charge of Wales. Every player had their ups and downs with Steve but despite his faults everyone had respect for him. He worked people very hard, although he was reasonably fair for most of the time. He brought professionalism to Welsh rugby and most people respected what he did for the Wales team. As well as taking on the job of national coach, he took on the task of helping set up the regional sides. Graham Henry tried to bring regional rugby in the whole time he was in Wales and Steve Hansen got it done in 18 months. Steve may have upset a few people along the way but I don't think there is any doubt that he improved Welsh rugby.

When he took over, there were a lot of players in the squad not giving their all in training. He made everyone realise that that was simply not good enough. Steve made decisions for the future, not the here and now, and some of those decisions came to fruition with that Grand Slam in 2005.

I certainly didn't finish my career with Wales as I had wanted to. I had endured a hard year that started with the preparations for the Rugby World Cup and was looking forward to touring Argentina and South Africa in the summer of 2004, under new coach Mike Ruddock. I was able to end my Cardiff career with a game against Edinburgh but it wasn't to be for Wales as I was advised by a specialist to rest a knee injury I had picked up against France.

On the whole, I was lucky with my injuries during my union career but they seemed to pop up every summer, preventing me from going on tour with Wales and it was so frustrating. I wanted to play, so I kept going, but it got worse and worse. I was always on the physio's table and then it was discovered I had torn ligaments. I didn't need surgery to fix the problem and was told it would heal of its own accord but it would take six to eight weeks for the bruising and the ligament to heal, which proved to be correct.

I was really looking forward to the tour as I'd been getting into some decent form towards the end of the year, and feeling good in myself. I'd earmarked the trip to really make a claim and was disappointed to have to pull out.

I was particularly looking forward to it as it marked the start of a new era, the end of the Steve Hansen reign and the start of the Mike Ruddock one. I had a great feeling about Mike from day one and it wasn't any surprise to me to see the way he improved the team, although I didn't think he would go and win the Grand Slam in his first Six Nations!

Even with Steve departing, it was crucial that Wales kept hold of Scott Johnson, the skills coach, and Andrew Hore, the fitness coach, for continuity, but then it was also important to bring in new blood and new ideas and that was to be Mike's role.

When I got my first cap against Argentina I wasn't quite ready for Test rugby, so I hoped to get the opportunity to show how much I'd improved as a player and how much we'd improved as a squad by returning to the same country.

Although I never got to work with Mike, at least I finished my international union career with a win, 44–10 over Italy, but it is a regret that I didn't know it was my last game when it started. Not going on the tour that summer forced me to sit down and think seriously about my future, discussions that finally ended with myself and Becky deciding it was time for a return back to the north of England and rugby league.

EIGHT

AUSSIE BOUND:
THE 2003 WORLD CUP

When I think of the 2003 Rugby World Cup, I have bittersweet memories. It was an unforgettable tournament but I felt the Wales team ended up underachieving.

Looking back, I have absolutely no doubt that the reason Wales did not go through to play France in the semi-finals of that World Cup can be summed up in two words: Mike Catt.

We've led matches at half-time in the past and sometimes not deserved to be in front, though we earned every precious point against England in that quarter-final to lead 10–3 at the break. But within five minutes of the restart, Will Greenwood was over and then a Jonny Wilkinson penalty put them 13–10 ahead.

In the second half, they just had too much possession and that amount of defending will lead to fatigue, mistakes and giving penalties away. You can't present someone like Jonny Wilkinson with that many penalties because he'll kick you out of the game. But it was Mike Catt's introduction in the second half that turned it England's way. It was crushing to watch his clearing kicks spiral deep into our territory. That sort of accuracy destroys you mentally and we were incredibly disappointed.

At our team meeting after the game the emphasis was all on taking the positives out of the match, including the three tries we scored, but England had a winning mentality: they never believed they would be beaten and in the end that mentality came to the surface to see them home.

It was hard to come to terms with the stark fact that we were out and heading home. This Wales squad had been together almost since May and we became more of a club team than the set-up you'd expect from an international side. Before we arrived in Australia, we went through a difficult pre-tournament schedule and I ended up playing in two of the four games. In 2003, we didn't have the normal autumn internationals due to the World Cup but we did have a build-up to Australia with games against Romania, England, Ireland and Scotland.

I missed the 54–8 win in Romania as Steve Hansen decided to try out some of the younger players. Gavin Henson contributed 24 points and a certain Shane Williams booked his place on the trip Down Under with a fantastic performance. The Romania game was Wales's first victory in 2003!

I think Steve Hansen identified the England game, the second in that series, as the match in which he would play his World Cup starting line-up. I missed out and was very disappointed, although through this series things didn't go to plan, with a 43–9 defeat to England at Cardiff followed by a 35–12 loss in Dublin.

The Ireland game was certainly a first for me as I was shown the yellow card. I got it for a head-high tackle but it was actually round the chest and simply slipped up. When I came off, I sat next to Steve Hansen and he said it was never a yellow card offence.

The England defeat hurt the squad. Any England defeat would, but this was worse as they fielded a team with very few of their World Cup players: to all intents and purposes it was a second string. I think this loss put question marks over a number of players and we entertained Scotland at the end of the series desperate for a victory to take to the World Cup. Luckily it came,

23–9, otherwise our confidence would have been in tatters.

Steve was very disappointed by that performance against England as a few players who he expected to show up, didn't. He came under a lot of pressure after the two defeats and there was a clamour for him to revert to his England team when Scotland came to town. But all credit to him, he said he had a plan to play three different sides and he was sticking to it!

People were suggesting that if we had lost to Scotland, Steve Hansen might have been sacked and I think that was true. He would have gone, even though we were about to go to the World Cup and the WRU would have pulled someone new in to take us to Australia. But we won that game and he picked a squad from the four games to go to the World Cup. I played myself into a starting position for the World Cup, the first choice side losing to England giving me a chance.

A win against Six Nations opposition was fantastic to take us Down Under. It helped us believe we could do well in Australia, giving the squad confidence – plus it was nice not to have to talk about losing streaks any more!

I know Steve's preparation techniques were criticised and some people even suggested we should have been playing for our regions in the run-up to the World Cup rather than staying in camps with Wales but, as Mike Ruddock showed in the 2005 campaign, a side like Wales benefits from more time together. To be fair, Steve never relayed the pressure he was under to the players. He protected us from that. His attitude was, 'Don't worry about the pressure I'm under', which was exactly the right perspective.

At the start of the warm-up games, I was beginning to doubt whether I would make the World Cup and although things got better as the series went on, culminating in that good win over Scotland, it was a huge relief when my name was read out in the squad. I thought the fact that I had missed the tour to New Zealand and Australia would count against me.

Going to a World Cup was one of the main reasons for me

making the switch from league to union. It was my major target from the moment I signed. Two years later and here I was going away with 29 blokes who were going to share a World Cup campaign. It was a very special time.

When we arrived in Australia, we went to Sydney for three days, which was important in building the great team spirit we had. From that point on, it was perfect because as a squad we enjoyed each other's company.

The World Cup was everything I had hoped for, everything I had expected. Australia, as they had shown in 2000 with the Olympics, knows how to put a show on and the World Cup was no different. Teams were adopted by the locals and they did everything they could to make this the best tournament to date.

I felt the people in Australia warmed to me a little bit more because of my rugby league background and their complete obsession with the game. While in Canberra we trained at the ground of the Raiders, the rugby league team, and it allowed me to do some catching-up with a few blasts from my past. Matthew Elliott, who was at Bradford when I played for Leeds, was the Canberra coach and Wayne Collins, whom I had played with, was youth coach there. But best of all, Brian Johnson, who had been my coach at Warrington all those years ago, was in charge of the Under-18s.

Although I was so far away from home, it was good to be in a place containing lots of people from my past. It was great to see Brian again and we spent a good session catching up and filling in the missing years. It was a bit like a home from home for me in Canberra. While I was in Australia, Graham Murray, my coach at Leeds, called me up and Edgar Curtis, who was the fitness coach, came to see me when we were in Sydney and went for a meal with myself and Adrian Morley.

Adding to the atmosphere, almost every game you played in was more or less in front of a full house. Any training sessions we had were fully organised and wherever we stayed was perfect. It was really done very professionally. We stayed in Canberra for most of the time, which was a pretty quiet place. We had our own apartments to live in and that allowed us to become settled.

We had been nagging the coaches to let us play golf from the moment we landed in Australia, as there were a few golfers in the team and, when they eventually did, it created a story I will never forget. The coaches only agreed to let us play if we used buggies and 15 to 20 of us ended up on one of the best inland courses in Australia.

We had a little competition and four of the front rowers, Gethin Jenkins, Duncan Jones, Adam Jones and Mefin Davies, decided to play together. They hadn't played that much, so basically came along for the ride (literally) and played a few shots. They went out first and when one of their balls went on the green, instead of parking the buggy up and walking to putt, they drove it straight onto the putting surface. After one wheelspin, they left the green in a terrible mess. We came after them, looking at this green saying, 'What's happened here?' The four guys never said a word about it and just shot off. The whole squad ended up with a fine of 3,000 Aussie dollars to put the green back together. All the culprits could say was, 'We didn't even know you couldn't go on the green in the buggy!' Forwards, eh, don't you love them!

It is almost impossible to compare the World Cups I played in, league and union. The one huge difference was the profile. In the 1995 League World Cup, we made a few headlines with Wales but it was nothing compared to the attention that surrounded this competition. The tournament was the talk of the country, and many others around the world.

There were a lot of unsung people in the Wales team at that time, like Brent Cockbain, one of the new faces in the squad. He was a tough character. Training was tough and Brent was one player who trained like he played. An Australian, he only got his residency qualification for Wales just before the World Cup and he added a lot to the squad. It was no surprise to me to see him still a major part of the team when Wales won the Grand Slam in 2005.

The moment that Steve Hansen saw him he liked him. Most people train at half-pace but with Brent everything is full out, training or playing, and that rubbed off on a lot of people. The two front rowers, Duncan and Adam Jones, were the same. They did a great job shoring up the scrum, something we'd had a load of trouble with in the previous years, so we had a really good mix.

Any good squad needs characters, players who will keep things bubbling along, players who can get a smile out of the rest at the right moment and this Wales team was no different. We had people like Gareth Thomas, who is a bubbly character, and Stephen Jones, who is always smiling. I don't think there was anyone who didn't get on. There was no divide between the forwards and backs. We had the experienced mixed in with the youngsters. Gareth Llewellyn was great – he was the oldest member of the squad but he often acted like the youngest. That sort of mix is very important.

I felt I had grown in terms of international rugby when we arrived at the World Cup. I was getting more confident in calling moves and felt completely comfortable with Steve Hansen, who gave me his full backing. Knowing that I had his confidence made a huge difference to me. The team became very competitive in a number of positions and I'm sure Steve had a number of tight, and tough, calls.

Looking around at the other groups, we were almost unique in that we didn't have an easy game in any one of our four pool matches, unlike England who faced two minnows, Georgia and Uruguay. They kicked off by beating Georgia 84–6, France put 61 points on Fiji and Scotland 32 on Japan, all sides ranked far below them, but for us our first game was completely different.

There was a fear that there might be a touch of ring-rustiness when we faced Canada in our first game on 12 October but the cobwebs blew away very quickly once we got on the pitch. There was certainly no time to ease ourselves into the tournament. We had everything to lose and nothing to gain, against a side ranked just below us.

Everyone was a bit nervous going into the game because it had felt like a long time coming. For me it had been most of my life, from the side-stepping around my caravan as a youngster. Playing for Wales in the World Cup was a day I had long dreamed about.

Having the pressure on right from the start must have suited us as we did a great job. Once we got into the game, we settled down and played some good rugby despite making a lot of mistakes. We scored five tries in our 41–10 victory, which gave us a bonus point, something we hadn't really thought about going for at the start, but when it came we realised that it could be precious.

The scoreline belied the fact that the Canadian game was a difficult one. They are the sort of team who can spoil it, slow it down and frustrate you if they need to. They like to kick to the corners and you can get caught off-guard by them now and again. We played them at the Millennium Stadium a year earlier and had to work really hard for that victory.

We knew it would be tough as they are a big, physical outfit, and we were right. We went behind initially but once we got in front we started to open up a little and scored some good tries. Defensively we were strong and caused them a lot of problems in attack.

The team spirit in the Wales side was very good. We'd gone through some tough times together and players who go through that are usually a lot stronger when they come out the other end. We were starting to see the light at the end of the tunnel. This was a significant time for the team, an exciting time as I could see the side start to transform.

Beating Canada in Melbourne, though, would mean nothing unless we followed it up with another victory over Tonga back in Canberra. If we'd lost to Italy, Canada or Tonga, we'd have had to have beaten New Zealand – and no one wanted to go into our last game of the pool stages needing to beat the All Blacks! We wanted to qualify before taking on New Zealand.

The build-up had been full and intense throughout the week, even though we saw Tonga as the easiest game in our group, but

I think we left plenty on the training ground. I was thrown into the starting XV at the last minute after Sonny Parker's back injury ruled him out, but that didn't affect me as I was prepared. Initially Steve Hansen told me I would be on the bench for Tonga, coming back into the team for the Italy game. Sonny thought he would be fine but pulled out on Thursday and Steve said I'd have to play. To be honest, I was delighted as I'm the sort of player who likes to get into a rhythm and play in every game. I don't like missing out.

On a personal note, it was a real thrill to receive our jerseys for the Tonga match from Australian rugby league legend Mal Meninga. I'd played against him a few years before and he was just a fantastic player, someone I watched in awe. Mal gave us some words of advice about what it takes to be a top side and the squad took a lot out of that, but the game was played completely differently to how we had planned. We expected it to be fast and open-paced but in the end the weather played its part and it turned into a physical, tight encounter. There wasn't much space and there was a lot of defending from both sides.

It was a scrappy affair and they took the game to us in the second half, but we felt in control for 90 per cent of the match without ever killing it off. We scored a try from Martyn Williams with 20 minutes to go after I threw out a long ball, which put us, very significantly, two scores ahead. We could relax a little more and eventually won 27–20.

There were mixed emotions afterwards. We were pleased with the win but disappointed with the way the game unfolded. We didn't expect the greasy surface and didn't adapt our game plan to compensate. As professionals you should be overcoming those obstacles and it demonstrated that despite the fact that we were winning we had an awfully long way to go.

Remarkably, Martyn Williams dropped a goal from under the sticks in that game, following in the footsteps of Zinzan Brooke, who famously kicked one against England in the 1995 World Cup. Steve Hansen's response was to say, 'Great drop goal, good thinking, but if you ever do that again while I am coach you will be dropped!' He said, 'I don't want my forwards kicking drop goals', and he was serious.

Martyn is one of those players who is always around the play and as he reads the game so well he is always going to have chances. We saw how crucial his try-scoring can be when he went over twice against France when Wales won the Grand Slam. If there is a slight breakdown, the chances are Martyn will be there. He's always been that way and has scored so many tries like that for Cardiff, so I wasn't surprised to see him attempt a drop goal and, considering how good a footballer he is, for it to go over.

We were down to the business end of the pool with our match against Italy and a place in the quarter-finals of the World Cup at stake. Italy were playing well at this point and, although they had lost to New Zealand, they scored 36 points to come back into the reckoning against Tonga.

Italy had beaten us in the previous Six Nations and were confident of knocking us off our perch. They'd been talking about that in the build-up to the World Cup.

Most of the talk about that game in Rome came from them. Our attitude was, 'That's history.' All of our focus was on the future.

Based on what happened in the warm-up games, Steve Hansen started with Ceri Sweeney at 10, although it was nip and tuck between him and Stephen Jones.

Even on the Thursday before the match on Saturday, everyone expected Stephen to play. But Ceri got the nod the day before the game. I don't know whether Steve Hansen changed his mind at the last minute but Stephen had been running the moves all week as if he was going to start. The first time Steve Hansen told us the side earlier in the week, he named them both. That in itself baffled us a little because we wanted to get the team finalised so we could concentrate on the game.

He might have spoken privately to Stephen and Ceri but we didn't know about that. Luckily, I had played with them both so it didn't really bother me. As it turned out Stephen came on in the 50th minute, so they almost shared the 10 jersey on that day.

Stephen entered the fray when we needed a boost and he kicked superbly out of hand. He relieved the pressure for us when we needed it. I remember one kick from a penalty which went around 70 metres down the field, taking the pressure right off. That sort of kick broke their hearts.

They had a number of older players who gave them experience and they tried to physically dominate us, but our forwards stood up to them. Mark and Dafydd Jones and Sonny Parker scored the only tries of a tense game, while I kicked 12 points in that 27–12 win to clinch our place in the quarters. We were always in control and I don't think we ever looked like losing.

We came to the tournament to make the quarter-finals and we were there, so we'd earned a night's relaxation and enjoyment. We were under a fair bit of pressure going in against Italy. We knew we'd be deemed failures if we came away with a defeat, and effectively drop out of the world's top eight sides. For a nation like Wales, with its rugby history, it was almost unthinkable that we wouldn't make the quarter-finals of the World Cup. The only thing that worried me was that we were still playing nervously. Only after we played the Italians did we loosen up. Following that victory we told each other we had nothing to lose. We had matches against two of the best teams in the world to look forward to and were determined to enjoy them.

After the Italy game, Zinzan Brooke said, 'Apart from their game against Canada, I haven't been very impressed with Wales. The only player that has really stood out has been Iestyn Harris. He has been one of the shining lights of the tournament so far and looks a class player.' It was very humbling to read that. Praise indeed.

After that Italian clash and before we took on England in the quarters, I sat in the stand and watched one of the most remarkable rugby matches I've ever seen when Wales went so close to beating the All Blacks.

We were already in the quarter-finals but a win over New Zealand would have seen us take on South Africa rather than England. I missed the game with a leg injury and Steve Hansen had decided to rest a number of players with the game against England on the horizon, so I may not have played anyway. At the time he said, 'Both (New Zealand and England) are huge games, but the second game has more riding on it. We have a responsibility to put our best and fittest side out for the quarter-final. If we had everyone fit and available we may have looked at things differently and put a couple more combinations out, but the crucial win over Italy has allowed us to plan with some foresight.

'We have two important games left and it's important everyone in the 22 does the job this week and then we will do another job next week. We don't have any less faith in the people we have picked.'

Steve had always said that if we won our first three games he would rest people. In the run-up to the All Blacks game I was sharing a room with Martyn Williams. Steve Hansen came into our room and told us he was very pleased with the way it had gone so far, and that he was giving us both a rest. He told us to go out and have a beer on the Friday night, relax, take it easy and look forward to the match against England. Once Steve had left I remember Martyn turning to me and saying that it was all very well resting us but if the team went out and played well against New Zealand we might not get back in, as he wouldn't be able to drop them. 'This could be the worst thing for me and you. We could end up missing out on the quarter-final,' he said. I took Martyn's words with a pinch of salt but it turned out to be true. When we played England, Martyn was left on the bench as Jonathan Thomas had played so well against New Zealand that Steve just couldn't leave him out.

At the time, I would rather have played against New Zealand. I felt the side had got into a bit of a rhythm and it's difficult when a coach says he's going to rest you. You are frustrated, but you know other players need and deserve their chance as well. As it turned out, the likes of Shane Williams, Stephen Jones and Jonathan Thomas really did take their chance against the All Blacks.

I know stories came out that the players had taken over, that they had shut the door on Steve Hansen and changed the game plan as they felt they had nothing to lose, but it wasn't like that. The way we wanted to play was the way we did play, it was just that we were a little more relaxed.

Rhys Williams was another one who missed out on the New Zealand game and then couldn't get back in the team after Gareth Thomas had come on at full-back and played a blinder.

I think Steve Hansen was supportive of the way they played and in fact they could, and maybe should, have won that game. Incredibly we led 37–33 with an hour gone, before Doug Howlett put New Zealand ahead with a try with just ten minutes remaining. We eventually lost 53–37 but you can imagine what a performance like that did for team spirit. It sent it sky high.

Sides like England and the All Blacks had a winning mentality in the World Cup. They think that no matter what happens in a game they can come back and win. It's a great feeling to have! I think that really came through when we played them both, going ahead against each one but failing to hold on to that lead. In both those games we could have had it sewn up and then you would have been talking about Wales in a World Cup semi-final, rather than on the plane home.

I think the atmosphere after that All Blacks game allowed us to go to Brisbane and take on England in the quarter-finals with confidence. We knew, of course, the team would change radically from the one that Steve Hansen had in his mind before that game and there were a number of nervous players in the Wales camp. There had to be changes to the team that Steve had planned, given the way the boys performed against one of the best teams in the world.

You have to worry about your place and Martyn and I were in

our room knowing that it would be hard to drop anyone after that performance. Steve Hansen picked his side pretty early in the week. We had a day off planned for Wednesday, so he picked it on Tuesday so people weren't worrying about it any longer than they needed to. I think everyone, whether they were in or out, appreciated that early call from Steve.

We had been used to sporting legends presenting us with our jerseys before games. We'd already had Glenn McGrath and Mal Meninga and before the England game the management were clever in using Brisbane rugby league legend Wally Lewis. Wally is so famous in Brisbane that he is just called The King. Wally Lewis was a name I knew very well. I knew how great a player he was.

All the people they brought in were guys who could put across the winning mentality and what it meant to have that mentality. I think that was a great idea as it ensured that it meant something to be presented with your shirt. Scott Johnson was the main instigator of getting these guys involved but it wasn't the first time Wales has done it as we had Mark Hughes and Scott Gibbs in the past.

Scott Johnson had a huge influence over the team. He did a lot of individual work with the players and always had time for people. So many of his ideas were well ahead of their time. Any time you needed help with any part of your game, he was there. I responded well to Scott, especially on the kicking side. You could compare him to Dave Alred and what he has done for England. Scott and Steve Hansen adopted the good cop, bad cop routine. Sometimes, if you felt you couldn't approach Steve, then Scott was there. However, I think deep down Scott was as hard a man, although he showed the good cop side to us more often. Andrew Hore was another key figure. He came in about two years before the World Cup so the squad could focus on the conditioning side of preparing for the tournament in Australia. Before Andrew, I think weight programmes and other conditioning had not been at the forefront of what Wales had done nationally. All of a sudden, Andrew came in with all these new ideas. He had a tough job, bringing in this new regime, as there was resistance from the clubs, but he did it extremely well. Andrew is a very persistent character and his persistence paid off.

He used to ring me up to ask if I'd done my weights, or a particular session. Speaking to the other players, I learned he was doing the same to them, so he must have had 40 or 50 players he was keeping in touch with personally every week. Every player will respond well to that sort of commitment. If you get someone ringing you asking you what you thought of a particular session and discussing it, you make sure you do your exercises and do them properly.

Andrew carried that commitment into the World Cup. He was always there doing extra sessions with one player or another. Crucially, he knew when you were too tired to do a session and how far he could push you. He made sure we got our eating habits right and obviously the long-term benefits brought dividends. In 2005, I know he was a big factor in Wales's Grand Slam season.

World rugby is at a level now where if one small thing is not perfect you have no chance of success. If you look at Ireland, England, Wales and France, they've got it right. Steve Hansen had a good team around him in Scott, Andrew and Clive Griffiths, who was back as defence coach, and you knew if there was ever a time when you wanted to work on something they were there for you. I think that was important.

The New Zealand match set us up for an epic quarter-final against England, a match we believed we could win. There was no question we now had the belief. The mood in the camp was buoyant after that performance against New Zealand, despite a few people missing out.

When you get to a quarter-final both teams are going to be nervous but we knew we were in a no-lose situation while there was a hell of a lot of pressure on them to win. We knew we could feed off that and turn it to our advantage. We resolved to go out and enjoy it. We decided not to worry about who we were up against. We set our minds on being as close to error-free as possible, while still trying to play an expansive game. We also believed the magnificent Wales fans would play their part. After watching England play Samoa in Melbourne, we knew we'd get a fair bit of the neutral support that probably wanted to see England lose, which couldn't hurt.

Against the likes of New Zealand and England, you've got to start well and that's what we were targeting. Although we were happy with what we'd achieved so far, no one in the squad was going to settle for the quarter-finals. We knew we had the ability to go further and, crucially, after the pool stages, even though we lost to New Zealand, we were on a roll. We were really enjoying the moment and wanted to keep playing well and progressing in the competition. We all knew that opportunities like this came rarely in a career and we all wanted to make the most of it.

As I wasn't selected for the New Zealand game, I was asked by Steve Hansen to become involved in the video analysis for England and present my findings back to the team. Some players complained about doing this sort of video analysis as they thought the coaches should be doing it, but the coaches always did their own work as well. Nevertheless, they were there, standing at the back, checking what we, the players, were saying was right.

I was put in charge of studying England's attack, looking at which way they attacked and how we could counteract it. I know they went on to win the World Cup but I thought they were quite predictable in attack. As a squad, we felt they relied heavily on Lawrence Dallaglio and his ball-carrying ability and I think it was very interesting to see how they fared without him in the 2004–05 season. We felt if England were ever struggling to get out of trouble, they would turn to Dallaglio. He was the one who'd take them ten yards forward to set up quick ball for their attackers like Robinson and Wilkinson. We believed if Lawrence Dallaglio didn't play, then England didn't play.

I think you only have to look at the World Cup final to see how important Lawrence was. A try down, it was Lawrence's run that set up Jason Robinson for the score that got England back into it.

To be fair, we did a really good job on Dallaglio right through our quarter-final – he didn't get anywhere, especially in the first half. We said that what people try to do is take him high, but he is very strong in the upper body so we weren't too bothered about getting a big shot on him. What was crucial was to get him low and get him early, and then we'd worry about the rest of it afterwards. The focus needed to be on him. England relied so much on Dallaglio in that tournament and I still believe if he hadn't played that day in Brisbane, it would have been us playing France in the semi-final and not England.

It was no surprise to me, although I know it was to some people, to see Dallaglio's name in the 2005 Lions squad. When he is at number 8 he gives a pack so much because he always breaks the gain line. I think he is a fantastic player and in Brisbane, because we did a job on him in the first half, England didn't know where to turn. They kicked a goal to go 3–0 ahead and then we completely took over. The try at the end of the first half was simply sensational as Shane Williams collected a long kick and went almost the length of the field to give us a 10–3 lead at the interval.

We were probably a little over-excited when we went in at half-time. It wasn't as bad as the Wales rugby league team all those years ago when we went ahead of Australia, but we were excited.

Apart from Dallaglio and Catt on that day in Brisbane, England's winning mentality was crucial. They arrived at the World Cup on the end of a very long winning run (they had only lost once in 20-odd games and that was with a second-string side in France) and that confidence can be worth a try start. They also had match winners like Jason Robinson. Throughout my career I've suffered a few times at the hands of Jason, and Brisbane was no different. He'd had a quiet game up to the start of the second half but then he came up with an incredible run to set up their only try from Will Greenwood.

In the first half, we were by far the better side but in the second we were out-kicked. As soon as we saw Mike Catt, we knew they were changing their game plan, and I don't think we were smart enough to react quickly enough. That comes down to the players but also to the coaching staff. They should have acknowledged that if England were going to change the way they played, we needed to adapt. That change was a credit to Clive Woodward. I think he recognised that we had worked out the way they played, which we had. We'd picked up the moves they were doing from a scrum. They used Ben Cohen heavily off scrums, on crash balls. We made sure we chopped him down straight away and they had no answer to that. Woodward saw that and realised he needed to make changes to keep them in the World Cup. And, to be fair, they did that.

Afterwards Clive Woodward came into our changing-room to thank us for the game. He said it was the toughest match they'd had all tournament and we really had them on the rocks. He added that if they did go on and win the World Cup, they'd look back at this game as a real turning point.

Steve Hansen, Scott Johnson, Andy Hore and Clive Griffiths thanked everyone and said we were all a credit to the country for what we had done. The game was on the Saturday, so with the plane home on the Monday the coaches told us to make sure we went out and enjoyed ourselves for a couple of days. That's what we did.

When we left the ground and got back to the hotel, there were probably around 1,000 Welsh people waiting for us. It felt like we had won. That support meant a lot to me and I know it did to the rest of the squad.

We had two really good days getting together for a night out and a day. We gave a few awards and had an excellent meeting. Some players carried on for a holiday around Australia but I was keen to see my family again.

Coming home was hard to take but it was made easier by seeing my family again. That was uppermost in my mind as I boarded the plane to come home. When we touched down, we went to another ceremony at The Barn at The Vale and again there must have been 1,000 to 1,500 people waiting for us.

My little girl, Catrin, was still talking nonsense when I left but when I got home she was forming proper sentences and looking forward to seeing her dad. Despite being at home and out of the World Cup, I think the squad could take a lot of pride from what we achieved, some of it coming to fruition 18 months later with the Grand Slam. It was upsetting in many ways because as we sat at home the tournament was still going on and we knew we could still have been out there. I watched the rest of the games but it was hard being a World Cup spectator. Against England we felt we were in a position to kick on but it just didn't happen. Looking back, it was an enjoyable tournament and I wouldn't give the memories up for anything in the world.

I watched the final. I know some Welsh people wanted Australia to win but I always wanted an England victory as I thought it was important for European rugby to finally have a winner and break the stranglehold of the southern hemisphere sides.

I also had a lot of respect for that England team. I thought they were gracious in victory against us. They could have easily been triumphalist but they weren't. I got the impression that they were a good bunch of guys. When they beat us, especially after the way they came back, they could have rubbed our noses in it but there was never any of that. When they were shaking our hands after the match, they were very gracious, thanking us for the game and appreciating how hard it had been.

The final of course came down to that incredible finish, Jonny Wilkinson kicking the winning drop goal with just 20 seconds to go. You see it time and time again and you know that Jonny Wilkinson is the one you'd want there, but when you look back at that move, they needed players like Dallaglio, Martin Johnson and Matt Dawson to drive them close to within Wilkinson's range. Again, as we knew he would be, Dallaglio was crucial moving them forward. They got great quick ball, so it meant the Australians had no chance of charging the kick down.

And you've got to say, especially as it was off his wrong foot, it was a brilliant kick. A lot of people forget that Jonny Wilkinson is left-footed but that winning drop goal came off his right. To kick any drop goal with 20 seconds to go in a World Cup final takes nerves of steel but to do it with your wrong foot, well . . . that's incredible. Trying to kick a goal with your wrong foot is damn near impossible, unless you have practised for hours and hours, which we all know Jonny has. His attention to detail and practising is legendary and I even noticed he took a few shots at goal when the teams were waiting for the start of extra time in that final. For him, I would think it was a way of steadying the nerves. It was what he knew best.

Throughout my career, I have probably practised my goalkicking four or five days out of any given seven, for around two to two and a half hours a day. I believe Jonny does a lot more than that!

At the time of the World Cup, I said I would remain a union player for the 18 months remaining on my contract, but things change. I knew the option on my contract was coming on the horizon and family reasons were making me consider a return to league. We'd had a great World Cup and we were looking forward to the Six Nations, followed by the tour to Argentina and South Africa.

Soon after the World Cup ended and in fact before the 2004 Six Nations began, news came through that another of my old rugby league buddies, Scott Gibbs, had decided to retire. Scott was a fantastic player in both rugby union and rugby league. As I was just starting to come through, he was really established in rugby league and I was lucky enough to play with him in a World Cup. He was a fantastic league player; strong, aggressive, he had everything needed to be a top-class performer. He was amazing to play with and tough to play against, then when he came back to rugby union he continued to be a fantastic player. He scored that superb try against England at Wembley in 1999 to win the game and that's probably what he's most remembered for.

But if I had to remember him for one thing, it would be as the ultimate professional. He'd been amazing in his training, he'd remained so strong. Whenever he'd been asked to perform, he'd done it, whether it was with Wales, the Lions, St Helens or Swansea. When he retired from international rugby in 2001, it was a huge loss to the Wales team and I'm sure he was a huge loss to Welsh rugby.

For me, at the end of the World Cup, there wasn't much point spending too long thinking about my future as there was no decision to be made at that time. The decision would have to come after the tour to Argentina and South Africa in the summer, which unfortunately I missed due to injury. I decided to play the 2004 Six Nations and then really consider what I was going to do. The memories of our time in Australia were, however, magnificent – days I will never forget.

NINE

BACK TO THE FUTURE

In an ideal world, my return to rugby league would have been at the start of the 2005 Super League season, but that would have meant spending from June 2004 until the following February without playing. That's a long time to be out of the game, particularly with the career of a professional rugby player being so short. I knew that when I retired I'd look back and regret missing almost an entire season and I didn't want to do that. I knew it would be tough but I was more than willing to jump in and play the games.

At a press conference on 1 July 2004, my signing for the Bradford Bulls was announced and, after watching my new club win at Castleford, I made my debut the following week at Odsal on 11 July.

On the field it was tough. The game had become extremely fast, a lot faster than it was three years before when I was playing for Leeds. The fitness levels are the same at both union and league but the type of fitness you need is very different. It's much more of a short, sharp regime in league: the ball is in play almost constantly, so obviously the training will be different. In union, there is far more stamina-based training which means working for longer periods, so after having played union for a while you certainly struggle to adapt.

During a rugby union international, the leading players may put in around 20 tackles: against Wigan I put in 42, so you can get some idea of the way they targeted me. In union, you train for longer and there is a lot more work, especially on the moves and the calls you might be using. As you can see from watching it, league is a far simpler game, so inevitably the training in union will be longer and usually more complicated. The weights are different. In union they use more wrestling weights to help you in the rucks and mauls. The running is also different: in pre-season you might do 1,500-, 1,000- or 800-metre runs, whereas in league it's more 10-, 20-, 30-metre shuttles.

We used to have to do about three tackles a week in training in league. I don't mean three tackling *sessions* but three good tackles on your opposite number, after we were put in grids. In union, they seemed obsessed with contact. I remember one contact session we did with Wales ended with Pontypridd's Geraint Lewis being out for six months with a cruciate knee injury and Cardiff scrum-half Richard Smith going off with an injured wrist. In league, we concentrate far more on skills. Surely it is better to focus on how to get round a team rather than just run contact drill after contact drill?

It was tough in those first games back in league. Outsiders looking into the sport would probably say, 'He's been back for three or four weeks so he should be back to his best.' But the human body is a strange thing. I think it takes 12 months to mould to a different regime. If you're doing something for three or four years, your body moulds to that system. Rugby union – fitness, weights and way you do things – is all different so your body naturally adapts to that. In rugby league, it's up and down off the floor, back and forward 10 metres, sprinting, stopping, sprinting, stopping. It takes your body 12 months to get into that.

It was only when I'd been back about a year that I felt my body was just about getting back into the kind of shape it needs to be in for rugby league. It can't happen over a couple of months, it's impossible. I compare it to a crash diet: as soon as you start eating normally, you put all your weight back on. It's got to be done over a longer period of time. Getting your body right for a specific kind of exercise is a similar kind of thing.

It took me 12 months to get it in union and 12 months to get it back in league but I knew that when I made my decision – I was willing to do that. In some games you want to do things but your body is that split-second behind. Towards the end of my second season, I felt I was getting back in sync. I didn't really consider having more time to prepare for my league debut with Bradford. Once you sign for a new club and you are fit, I think you have to try and play.

Certainly in the 2004 season there were games in which I struggled. It was enough just getting used to the constant up and down off the floor. It was frustrating because I felt I had a lot more to give but, physically, I just couldn't. I couldn't wait to play and it was just a matter of me settling in at the club. I watched them win at Castleford and then I was selected on the bench for the match against the Wakefield Trinity Wildcats. I only came in so soon because Paul Johnson had been ruled out for six weeks after breaking his right arm.

I suppose I was lucky that the game was at Odsal. I had itchy feet and was desperate to get on, but Brian wanted to ease me in. It was a good introduction back into the game when I came into the game after 53 minutes. It was already won, so there wasn't a massive amount of pressure. I still felt a tiny bit lost but I knew that wouldn't last for long. We played most of the match with 12 men after Karl Pratt was sent off following a mass punch-up. It's always difficult when you are down to 12 men and it felt a little bit strange playing on the wing but I had to play a defensive role as the Wildcats threatened an upset. We eventually won 36–26.

Over the first few weeks, I knew it was simply a matter of clinging on and doing the best I could. I was in the starting line-up for the next match at Wigan at stand-off and throughout the game the Wigan players were shouting 'Run at him! Run at him!' This gives you some idea of the way I was being treated. Even 20 yards away, you could hear them shouting, 'There he is, get at him.' Sometimes they even ran across the field to get at me and when that happened for the first time I knew I was in for a long day at the office. The only way I could react to the Wigan players was to just smile and make sure I made a lot of tackles, although we ended up losing 32–16.

In the old days, I might have enjoyed a laugh and a joke with the Wigan players afterwards but now – in the fully professional era – you don't seem to have the chance for a pint and a chat after the game. Again, I don't think it was anything personal, they thought I was a weak link in the team. It wasn't about me coming back to play league, it was about Wigan thinking they had someone they could target. Both Brian and I knew it was coming but he didn't have any doubts I could handle it, and that gave me additional confidence.

I knew the opposition would see me as a weak player as they doubted that my fitness levels would be the same as they were when I left. For the first three or four weeks I did put in an extra fitness session or two, just to get used to the ups and downs, but I didn't do anything else out of the ordinary to prepare. I could obviously have done without people targeting me but it was exactly what I expected. In the same way as the fans booed me, when I was targeted on the field it showed a little bit of respect for me. I knew it was coming and if they had ignored me it would have been worse.

My first points came in our 44–16 win over London, my third game back, but more importantly the victory took us into the top four of Super League. We ran in eight tries, two of them from Lesley Vainikolo, and I managed to kick a couple of goals.

After that game Brian Noble said, 'Iestyn has been thrown in at the deep end but he has done everything we wanted of him.'

Towards the end of August, five games into my comeback, we were due to play the Leeds Rhinos at Headingley. Brian came up to me a few days before the match and asked me if I wanted to give the game a miss. He said no one would think any the worse of me if I did, but it took only a couple of seconds for me to turn down Brian's offer. I knew exactly where he was coming from but I've never been one to duck a challenge. I knew I'd have to go back to play at Headingley one day, so why not straight away? It was definitely a case of trying to get this one out of the way sooner rather than later.

Of course it turned out to be a hostile day but I have many, many good friends at Leeds and it was all about an old boy going back to play against his former club. I didn't feel the songs, the booing and the catcalling were anything personal. As a supporter you want your team to do well and will do anything to try and make it happen. The treatment on the field I got at Leeds was no worse than what I received at other rugby league grounds on my return. The friends on the playing staff at both Warrington and Leeds hadn't changed. You are hardly going to fall out with a mate just because he has joined a rival team. I wouldn't do that to a friend of mine and I wouldn't expect them to do that to me. I never had any problems with any fans on an individual basis. Obviously when they are together in a crowd, the boos will come but in a way I find that a compliment. If they weren't bothered about me they wouldn't target me.

Deciding not to go back to Leeds wasn't personal. The club and I had shared so many glory days, there was no way I wanted my relationship with that club and its fans to become sour. On my way into the ground I received perhaps one negative comment, compared to ten positive ones, and I think there was an element of respect from some people at the club that I hadn't ducked out of actually playing the game, as it would have been easy to feign an injury. Obviously things changed a little when the fans were all together on the terraces and the songs started up. It was exactly what I had expected, but it was all in good spirit. I loved my time at Leeds but you move on and things change.

On the field I knew the players would try to knock my head off from the start, so I was determined to get a few blows in first. That game was built up as my return and we probably played our worst game of the year. They thumped us and it turned into a long day for me as the crowd was on my back for the whole match.

It wasn't the first time I had been back to Headingley since leaving, as I returned for a testimonial match for my former teammate, Francis Cummins, while I was in union. I didn't play in the game but just kicked some balls at half-time. People were very supportive of me, many asking me if I would come back. They were saying they wanted me back, but it just didn't feel right for me to go back to Leeds.

I didn't have any real expectations for that first season but it almost ended in glory as we made the Grand Final, and you hardly need to guess who we were playing in that 2004 Grand Final. Whether you are a fan of rugby league or not, it was inevitable that if we made it we would face Leeds. Sport always seems to be like that.

We finished runners up to Leeds in Super League, although we were nine points behind them. In the play-off we were due to meet them in the qualifying semi-final at Headingley.

We got off to a great start, Shontayne Hape scoring two tries in the first 15 minutes. I was lucky enough to set up the position for the opening score, with Paul Deacon spotting that the Rhinos were short on the left and helping create an opening for Hape to crash through. Lesley Vainikolo claimed his 38th try of the year, which took us to an amazing 26–12 victory, the first time Leeds had been beaten at Headingley all season. As there was so much at stake in this semi-final game, the crowd didn't seem to be on my back so much. That win took us to Old Trafford, Bradford's fifth Grand Final in seven years.

Lesley Vainikolo is a fantastic player. I would certainly rather have him in my side than playing against me. In 2004 he struggled a little bit with injuries but when he is fit and on form he is close to unstoppable. You don't realise what a good player Lesley is until you play with him. He is a freak of nature, so strong and quick, he's almost impossible to stop when he is in full flight. I played against him once for Wales in the Rugby League World Cup, when he played for New Zealand, and there was talk of him turning out for Tonga in the 2003 Rugby Union World Cup. There was a really serious threat of him playing in Australia, but it never happened.

When he runs at full flight you wouldn't want to be in front of him. But, like most South Sea Islanders, he is a great man to have in your squad. Nothing bothers him. In many ways, he reminds me of Inga Tuigamala, laid back off the field, a lovely guy, but on the field he becomes a different animal altogether. Any side in the world would want him. In 2005, there was some talk of Lesley following in my footsteps and making the move to union, perhaps with Gloucester, but I was delighted to see him sign a new deal with Bradford.

It was very strange to play against Leeds in the Grand Final but that's one of the things you have to get used to in professional sport. It was a huge surprise for me to make such good strides in my first season and it was clear to me that I had made the right decision, following the support coach Brian Noble gave me during the season and in the run-up to this game.

Before that Grand Final, Brian was kind enough to say, 'I didn't think Iestyn would be as impressive as he is now. I thought that would be next year, with an off-season in him and a chance to get to know the players. But he has fitted in really quickly. I suppose it's like riding a bike, he's got up to speed pretty quickly.'

As the Rhinos had finished on top of the table, they were given a second chance, leaving them to beat Wigan, which they did to set up another meeting with us in the final.

In 1998, on my last appearance in a Grand Final, I was captain of the Leeds team that lost 10–4 to Wigan, so it seemed strange to be playing them at Old Trafford in 2004. The Leeds fans always have a few words for me and it was no different this time. All I could do, as I have always done, is try to keep them quiet by playing good rugby.

As I played more games, I felt myself getting a bit fitter and before the Grand Final, I reached the stage where I was playing towards my best.

It was going to be hard to beat a side as strong as Leeds were in 2004 twice in quick succession. At that stage of the year, the two teams were very close and for either side to win both those games would have been very tough.

In that Grand Final, we dropped a lot of ball, as they did. It was a very nervous affair but we just didn't play well. It was tight, though, with Leeds holding a slender two-point lead for the majority of the second half before they clinched the game in the 74th minute with a try from Danny McGuire.

Overall, in 2004, Leeds were the best side in the competition and they proved that by beating us 16–8. It meant a huge amount to that Leeds team because, as the *Yorkshire Post* pointed out, only two members of the team that completed the victory were born the last time Leeds claimed the title in 1972. I thought Leeds deserved it but it was a bitter pill to swallow for me and the Bulls. On the day, they were probably slightly the better side. To be involved in the Grand Final in that first season back was massive. It's frustrating to lose, but to be involved in that kind of atmosphere at that kind of ground was the reason I came back.

I wasn't kicking in that first season as it is something Paul Deacon, my half-back partner, has done for some time and in my first year back it was one pressure I was relieved to be without. If asked, of course, I would have done it but perhaps it was easier to come back without those responsibilities, although, in 2005, when Paul was injured I did take over. But it didn't bother me not to be kicking.

It seemed that no sooner was I back in league than we had a massive Test series against New Zealand and Australia, the first Tri-Nations. What a way to make a comeback to international rugby league!

In November, I was named in Brian Noble's Great Britain squad for the tournament, after having played only 13 matches for the Bulls since returning from rugby union. Although Brian was Bradford coach as well as being in charge of the national side, when I was negotiating with him to come back to league we never talked about Great Britain.

When I went to union, I thought I'd played my last league international, so it was a great feeling to be back. I won nine caps during my first stint in league, the last being in the Tri-Nations series, in Auckland, in 1999. I was lucky to have the backing of Brian Noble on my return to the international stage. I needed to break back into the Great Britain set-up as soon as I could and I am very grateful to Brian. He was very kind to me in the run-up to that Tri-Nations series saying, 'These sort of chances come around once in a lifetime. I rate Iestyn up there with the likes of Andy Farrell and Paul Sculthorpe. He is a very talented individual who made the move back from union to league look far easier than I anticipated. He was concerned about his tiredness but I think I convinced him that to be part of what we hope will be a special series would be good for him. If he feels he is tired during the series, we will rest him, but he's a talented lad who could help us win the tournament.'

Brian was right. I was feeling a little tired as I had been playing rugby, non-stop, for almost 18 months, but I knew it wouldn't be long before I had a rest. It was such a long season for me. When we started out on the Tri-Nations series it was my 16th month without much of a break. I had to stay mentally focused and was trying to make a big impact on the play-offs, which were the most important thing for me. However, I was so happy to be part of the Great Britain set-up again – although I must admit to having second thoughts about actually taking part, especially after the play-offs had already extended my season.

I wasn't in the team to face Australia in our opening match at the City of Manchester Stadium, which we lost 12–8, but I was on the bench for the next one, against New Zealand at the Galpharm Stadium, Huddersfield. That was a really tough encounter, with the Kiwis taking control early on and going in at half-time 12–2 ahead. We didn't panic and maybe that's a new thing for us because in the past we have when we've gone behind. Even at half-time, we were confident we could win and battled back in the second half, scoring 20 unanswered points to claim victory and register our first Tri-Nations win.

I didn't think it was a particularly fast game and was able to cope with the pace but I was surprised just how physical it was, even in the last quarter. Super League, particularly the play-offs, is very nearly international standard now and the step up isn't as big as you might think. I even got my chance to do some kicking, following Andy Farrell and Paul Sculthorpe, landing two goals; the first, a penalty, was the first goal kick I'd taken for about three months.

It was hard to adjust to league at first, particularly defending, but I've played the game since I was 17, so I was always confident the change wouldn't be too hard to make. Many of the old faces I left when I moved to union three years before were still around and in that first international game it gave me the chance to renew my rivalry with old friend, and now club teammate, Robbie Paul.

New Zealand are always a very physical side, whatever code you're playing, and stopping their forwards was the key. I tried to drum into the rest of the squad how much we had to watch Robbie, who's an exceptional player in any side he plays for. Like Lawrence Dallaglio for England in the union game, we knew we had to stop Robbie early in the game. To be honest, everyone knew that if we could inflict some pain on him we'd slow them down.

In the Tri-Nations final, we faced Australia at Elland Road, Leeds, which proved to be one of the most painful matches of my international career. There was a full house and lots of expectation but the Australians treated it as just another game. They blew us away in an incredible first half and after 20 minutes we were saying to ourselves, 'What's happening here?' You'd smash into them but they would just throw the ball over their heads, it would stick and they'd score a try. We just couldn't stop it. I don't think they dropped a ball in the opening ten minutes. They would just take three tackles, kick, then sprint downfield. I don't think our front row touched the ball. It was the best 40 minutes you'll see from a side and they scored seven tries, winning 44–4. I couldn't bring myself to watch the tape afterwards.

That finally brought to a close my first season back in rugby league and I could at last have a rest and reflect on an incredible year and a half.

On 19 March 2005, I made sure I reserved my place in front of the television to see Wales clinch their first Grand Slam since 1978 by beating Ireland, 32–20. That Six Nations became an unforgettable event for all Welshmen, myself included, and I was so pleased for the team. I was very confident they would beat England in the opening game but before a ball was kicked not even I would have dreamed of anything as great as what unfolded over the next few weeks. Those guys deserved the good times because over the previous three years, there have been some bad times, going back to when they lost to Italy in Rome. Every man and his dog was jumping on the backs of all the players. But things had changed, the set-pieces were very good and all over the park they seemed very dangerous. They looked very, very good and tough to stop.

Memories of my move to rugby union came back in March 2005 when it was confirmed that Andy Farrell would follow players like myself, Jason Robinson and Henry Paul in switching from league to union. He was a couple of months short of his 30th birthday and was leaving it very late to make the transition. He will be almost 32 by the time of the next World Cup, an age when most people are coming to the end of their careers.

Andy has been targeted by England coach Andy Robinson as a key figure in his plans to defend the World Cup in 2007, and all I would hope is that he is given the same sort of introduction to the sport as Jason Robinson was and not me. Andy should be eased not just into the England team but also into the England squad. Time is the key, as he has a brand new sport to learn.

Anyone who has seen Andy play would be in no doubt about his abilities but Andy Robinson must go slowly with him rather than following my example. I went straight into a struggling Wales team which had lost a lot of players due to retirement and that made it very difficult for me. People need to bear in mind once Andy starts playing rugby union that what they mustn't do is use him as a scapegoat for what has happened before he either became a union player or became an England player. A lot will depend on the kind of support he gets from the people around him, particularly at his club Saracens.

I don't think you'll see many more people going from league to union, because the players in league have been professional for so long and I think the game's just going to get better and better. I was one of the first to go full time at a young age but now you're getting youngsters coming through who have been full time since the age of 14 and 15. They're not rugby players, they're athletes, pure athletes who have adapted to the game of rugby league.

I think there's more of a threat from Australia picking up our best players than union. I'm not saying the odd one or two might not go but I don't think there's any threat to the game because a lot of players simply can't adapt to union.

In Wales they love rugby league. If you walk into a pub on Friday or Saturday night, unless there's rugby union on another channel, you'll find them watching Super League. There's a lot of respect for rugby league, particularly from the players. When we were in camp with the Welsh squad on Friday nights, there'd be ten to twelve of the players watching it on Sky and they all had their favourite teams.

As for a Welsh team in Super League, that's a difficult one. It's very tribal in Wales. You have to live there to understand it. If you had a team in Cardiff, then no one from, say, Pontypridd would go and watch Cardiff, and vice versa.

I think the only way would be to base it in one place, give it the name of that place and you'd get a nucleus of people, around 10,000, watching a Super League side. If you tried to capture the whole of Wales by calling a team the Welsh Dragons, or something like that, you've got no chance, but the game could be quite big there.

Another fascinating development is to see England linking up with the Leeds Rhinos and Wales with St Helens to experience each other's training and preparation. It says much for the vision and foresight of Andy Robinson that he made a big point of going and training with the Rhinos as his side prepared for the 2005 Six Nations. I think it's crucial for all sports teams to have as much variation as possible in their training routines and to go to league, in an attempt to learn a few things, says so much about how good a coach Andy Robinson is. A few decades before, all the players would have been banned for attending such a session. Thank goodness things have moved on a little since the bad old days when league and union hated each other.

I can confirm that there is a healthy respect between the two sports and if each of us can do something to help the other take on the southern hemisphere, then why not? Having heard from a few of the England union players, it seems that the thing they enjoyed most about league training was the lack of contact and the focus on skills.

I found the biggest difference between the two codes was the intensity. In union, the European Cup was fantastic but the Celtic League was so indifferent. You'd have a real tough game against a Welsh region, then you'd play an Irish province who'd send a third-string side over and you'd win by 30 or 40 points. Or because we had so many players in our squad, the coaches would rest players for the easier games. So it would be two weeks on, two weeks off, then you'd go to Wales training and start playing internationals. The Celtic League games were still going on while you were away, then you'd come back and play a couple of European games. It was so inconsistent. I was tearing my hair out because I'd been used to playing 26 to 28 games a year constantly at the highest level in Super League where everyone put their best sides out to compete and try to get into the top six.

The whole concept of the Celtic League was to get your European spot but as there were only four regions it didn't really matter where you finished because all four qualified. If you played Leinster you thought you'd be up against Brian O'Driscoll and other players of that calibre, but you'd look at the team sheet and it would be full of Under-21s. That wasn't right – it should be the best against the best but it never was.

The first year I was there, before the formation of the Celtic League, Cardiff were one of 11 teams playing in the Welsh-Scottish League. I remember playing against Caerphilly, the bottom club, in one of the last games of the year and there was one man and his dog on the sidelines. You could hear the solitary claps from the odd spectator. It was like being back in the A team at Warrington. Of course, not a lot of games were like that. Cardiff was a big city club and had a good following but some of the Welsh teams struggled.

The 2005 season was to be my first full season back in league but it didn't start as well for Bradford and we struggled due to a number of factors, although my faith in the squad was not shaken. When players retire or leave, you have lulls at clubs and I think that's what happened at Bradford. The likes of Mike Forshaw and James Lowes had both retired and Paul Anderson moved on. You've got to have that restructuring every two or three years and that's what happened with Bradford. We made a stuttering start to 2005, losing our opening two league games to Wakefield and Widnes, but we did a similar thing in 2004 and still made the Grand Final! We were at sixes and sevens but we knew we would click.

You always go through stages in your career when you're in a good side and you can't understand why you are not playing well, but there was never any panic.

After those early losses, we bounced back with a 28–27 victory over Wigan at the JJB Stadium but although we continued to pick up in the Super League, our Challenge Cup campaign ended with a 26–24 defeat at Hull.

Our hopes of a fourth final appearance in six years were scuppered by another dismal first-half display. We fought back from 18–0 down to beat London in the Super League the week before and we almost did it again at Hull after trailing 20–0 at the break.

Nothing, though, not even missing out on another Challenge Cup final would make me regret my decision to return north or the fantastic time I had in union. In many ways, I have lived a dream in my professional rugby career, both in union and league, but getting to my late 20s, I think its time to consider what I'm going to do when I hang up my boots. Thinking about it when you're 33 is too late and 25 is too early, so now is the time to decide which direction I want to go.

I'd like to stay in the game but I'm no fool, there are thousands who want to but probably only tens of people who do. Maybe I'll go into the media or coaching. We'd like to set up a business for my wife to run over the next four years and I intend to do a sports degree at some stage.

You can't put all your eggs in one basket, it's a fickle game. Look at someone like Andy Goodway – he was Wigan and Great Britain coach, the world was at his feet, but two minutes later he was out of a job.

Maybe over the next year I will decide fully what I want to do. But I still want to win a Grand Final and I've got four years at the top level to try and do that – I'm sure I will.

All I hope now is that the dream can continue and give me more unforgettable days, both on and off the pitch.